Studies in Canadian Geography

Études sur la géographie du Canada

Edited by /Sous

The North   Le Nord

Edited by/Sous
la direction de
William C. Wonders

published for the 22nd International Geographical Congress
publié à l'occasion du 22e Congrès international de géographie
Montréal 1972

University of Toronto Press

© University of Toronto Press 1972
Toronto and Buffalo

ISBN 0-8020-1923-4 (Cloth)
ISBN 0-8020-6164-8 (Paper)
Microfiche ISBN 0-8020-0260-9

Printed in Canada

Contents

Foreword

The publication of the series, 'Studies in Canadian Geography,' by the organizers of the 22nd International Geographical Congress, introduces to the international community of geographers a new perspective of the regional entities which form this vast country. These studies should contribute to a better understanding among scholars, students and the people of Canada of the geography of their land.

Geographical works embracing the whole of Canada, few in number until recently, have become more numerous during the last few years. This series is original in its purpose of re-evaluating the regional geography of Canada. In the hope of discovering the dynamic trends and the processes responsible for them, the editors and authors of these volumes have sought to interpret the main characteristics and unique attributes of the various regions, rather than follow a strictly inventorial approach.

It is a pleasant duty for me to thank all who have contributed to the preparation of the volume on the North. A special thanks is due to: Mr R.I.K. Davidson of the University of Toronto Press; Mr Geoffrey Lester who guided the Cartography Laboratory of the Department of Geography, University of Alberta in preparing all the illustrations; the Canadian Association of Geographers for its financial support; and the Executive of the Organizing Committee of the 22nd International Geographical Congress. Finally I wish to thank Dr William Wonders, professor of geography at the University of Alberta, for having accepted the editorship of this volume.

LOUIS TROTIER
Chairman
Publications Committee

Avant-propos

Par la publication de cette série d''Etudes sur la géographie du Canada,'
les organisateurs du 22e Congrès international de géographie ont voulu
profiter de l'occasion qui leur était donnée de présenter à la communauté
internationale des géographes une perspective nouvelle des grands ensembles régionaux qui composent cet immense pays. Ils espèrent que ces
études contribueront aussi à mieux faire comprendre la géographie de
leur pays aux Canadiens eux-mêmes, scientifiques, étudiants ou autres.

Les travaux d'ensemble sur la géographie du Canada, peu nombreux
jusqu'à récemment, se sont multipliés au cours des dernières années.
L'originalité de cette série provient surtout d'un effort de renouvelle-
ment de la géographie régionale du Canada. Les rédacteurs et les auteurs
de ces ouvrages ont cherché moins à inventorier leur région qu'à en inter-
préter les traits majeurs et les plus originaux, dans l'espoir de découvrir
les tendances de leur évolution.

C'est pour moi un agréable devoir de remercier et de féliciter tous ceux
qui ont contribué d'une manière ou d'une autre à la réalisation de cet
ouvrage sur le Nord. Il convient de mentionner les membres du Comité
d'organisation du 22e Congrès international de géographie; M. R.I.K.
Davidson, des Presses de l'Université de Toronto; l'Association canadienne des géographes; le Ministère des Affaires indiennes et du Nord;
le département de géographie de l'Université de l'Alberta, à Edmonton,
dont le Laboratoire de cartographie a préparé toutes les illustrations de
cet ouvrage sous la direction habile et dévouée de M. Geoffrey Lester. Je
remercie enfin M. William Wonders, professeur de géographie à l'Université de l'Alberta, d'avoir accepté d'assumer la direction de cet ouvrage.

LOUIS TROTIER
Président du
Comité des publications

Preface

Of the several geographic regions of Canada the most distinctive is probably the North. In the entire world only one other nation, the USSR, possesses a region comparable in terms of either absolute or relative area involved. Similarities exist, but there also are major differences in both the physical and the cultural characteristics of these two northlands. In this volume we have attempted to set out some of those features which impart an individuality to the Canadian North nationally and internationally. At the same time the organization of the volume has followed an overall plan similar to that of the other volumes in this series, since the North is an integral part of that fascinating mosaic which constitutes Canada.

An overriding problem for the contributors to this volume has been the vastness of the region involved – more than the combined area of all other five regions of Canada included in this series. Within such a great area, almost 'continental' in scale, major differences in geographic characteristics might be expected and, in fact, do occur. The problem therefore of compressing the essential features to the degree required to meet publication limitations has been particularly difficult in the case of the North. Nevertheless the attempt has been made.

Until relatively recently the North often has been treated in sweeping generalizations, reflecting the limited knowledge of the region. Drawing upon the increasing amount of accurate factual information available in the postwar years, Bird sets out the physical characteristics of the North which make it such a distinctive region. In doing so he not only explains the background to many present environmental conditions but stresses also the diversity within the region which often is not appreciated.

One of the peculiarities of the North is that, while the term is widely associated with Canada and is commonly used among all Canadians, there is little agreement on its geographic definition. Hamelin examines this problem and suggests a solution to it in his treatment of the ecumene of the Canadian North. He also sets out major subregions within it as defined in his proposed VAPO unit classification.

While transportation was the means by which the initial unification of Canada was achieved, its presence or absence in the North has been no less vital in the integration of that immense region within the national framework. Marsden summarizes the essential features of the various transportation media existing within the region, with some speculation on the future. Regrettably, the closely related communications facilities could not be included because of space limitations.

Of the various economic activities associated with the North none is more characteristic than mining – indeed over much of the region it is the only economic activity. It is appropriate therefore that it be given special attention by Tough in this volume.

Population in northern Canada has many distinctive aspects as compared with the other regions of the nation. The total numbers of people are extremely low considering its area; the urbanizing process so marked elsewhere has been long delayed in this region, and the relative numbers of indigenous peoples in its population is higher than elsewhere in Canada. These and several other facets are dealt with by Bone.

The sheer size of the North in a highly political world has important repercussions for Canada as a nation, both internally and internationally. Stager reviews the role of the North politically at the present time against a brief historical perspective, and speculates on its prospects. The final chapter attempts to provide an overview of the Canadian North in its relations to the rest of the country and to extend this into the future. In this it suggests that the region offers a unique opportunity for evolving new approaches to development.

Because of space limitations, maps and bibliography have had to be severely restricted, at times despite the protestations of individual authors that no further reduction was possible. Text also has been curtailed beyond the point that some contributors felt to be the absolute minimum. I must assume responsibility in such cases and hope that the quality of content and presentation has not suffered excessively from the editorial pencil. I wish to express my personal appreciation to the contributors to this volume for the time and care they have donated towards the success of the 22nd International Geographical Congress. The encouragement and assistance of the general editor of the series, Professor L. Trotier, have been most helpful.

In the final production of this volume several skilled specialists of the Department of Geography, University of Alberta, have played an indispensable role: G.A. Lester and his cartographic staff; J. Chesterman; Miss J. MacLeod. To them I extend the appreciation of all the contributors.

University of Alberta
21 January 1972

W.C.W.

1 The Physical Characteristics of Northern Canada

J. BRIAN BIRD

The physical environments of northern Canada are dominated by long periods of intense winter cold, winter darkness (although not absolute in the extreme southern sector) and, conversely in summer, continuous daylight, and the presence of freezing and near freezing temperatures in the ground throughout the year. The overall northern environments are more complex and may be described in terms of climate, landforms, soils, ground moisture, and vegetation. Macro- and mesoclimates are largely independent of other environmental factors, excepting topography; similarly the larger landforms are usually independent since they are inherited from the past environments although in detail they are being modified today. In contrast microlandforms, microclimate, soils, vegetation, ground moisture, and temperature are closely dependent, changes in one element leading quickly to modification of several or all of the others. Each will be described in turn, but their interdependence should never be forgotten.

INHERITED LANDSCAPE FEATURES

Structural History

The geological and physiographic core of the North is the Canadian Shield. The exposed Shield is roughly circular in plan with a diameter of 3500 km (2200 mi); two-thirds lies within the North. The irregular northern boundary crosses the southern arctic islands, while in the west the margin is a sweeping contact that cuts through Great Bear, Great Slave, and Athabasca lakes. The exposed Shield is part of a larger unit of Precambrian rocks of which buried sections in the north reach Parry Channel and on the west side, the foothills of the Cordillera.

The Canadian Shield grew in geological complexity through several orogenies in the Precambrian, Granites and granite gneisses constitute no less than 80 per cent of the surface, with jointing imparting a characteristic topographic grain to the landscape. Within the granite gneiss areas are folded, but less highly metamorphosed sediments. Rocks of this unit underlie the Labrador Trough south of Ungava Bay and the Povungnituk Hills in extreme northern Quebec. In strong contrast with the rocks already described are flat-lying to gently folded sandstones, limestones, and dolomites, mainly of mid-Proterozoic age which overlie the older Shield rocks in the Thelon and Athabasca plains, in the hills north of Great Bear Lake, and in central Victoria Island. Volcanic rocks are frequently associated with these sediments and thick basalt flows form magnificent cuesta scenery around Coronation Gulf.

Shallow transgressive seas covered much of the present exposed Shield during the Ordovician. Limestone and dolomite of this age are preserved today north and west of the Shield and small outliers that survive on the Shield in Quebec and Keewatin suggest strongly that the Shield was once covered completely by these rocks. Subsequent deposition continued locally on the northern and western margins of the Shield. Today Palaeozoic and Mesozoic rocks form extensive sedimentary lowlands, scarplands, and plateaus bordering the Shield.

While these events were occurring, two less stable geosynclinal areas were developing. In the far west, the complex Cordilleran geosynclines experienced main folding in the Triassic (Tahltanian) in the Yukon Plateau, and the late Cretaceous and early Tertiary (Columbian and Laramide) elsewhere in the northwest. Meanwhile the northern edge of the continent, beyond Parry Channel, saw the creation of the Innuitian province. Following sedimentation, the Ellesmerian orogeny in late Devonian and Mississippian times formed the Parry Islands, central Ellesmere and northern Ellesmere fold belts. A regional depression, the Sverdrup Basin, in the centre of the Queen Elizabeth Archipelago accumulated sediments from Lower Carboniferous to Upper Cretaceous and Tertiary. The basin then experienced folding, faulting, and the emplacement of piercement (gypsum) domes during an orogeny that corresponded with the Laramide in the west. Finally, along the shores of the Arctic Ocean from the Alaska border to Meighen Island there was a period of deposition in late Tertiary or early Quaternary times which left sands, gravel, and silt of the Beaufort formation.

The orogenic belts no longer correspond with contemporary mountain ranges everywhere in the north, either because of denudation or because of erosion and subsequent burial beneath younger sediments as in part of the Sverdrup Islands. However, tectonic activity in the mobile sectors of the Canadian North continued into the Tertiary resulting in a youthful geological landscape. In contrast, the major elements of the Shield scen-

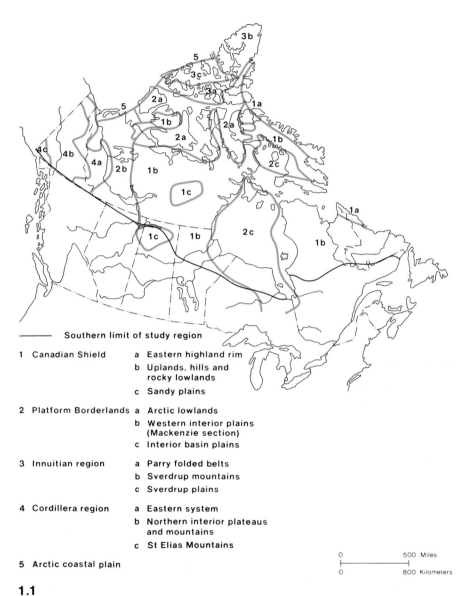

——— Southern limit of study region

1 Canadian Shield   a Eastern highland rim
                            b Uplands, hills and
                               rocky lowlands
                            c Sandy plains

2 Platform Borderlands a Arctic lowlands
                            b Western interior plains
                               (Mackenzie section)
                            c Interior basin plains

3 Innuitian region   a Parry folded belts
                            b Sverdrup mountains
                            c Sverdrup plains

4 Cordillera region   a Eastern system
                            b Northern interior plateaus
                               and mountains
                            c St Elias Mountains

5 Arctic coastal plain

0   500 Miles
0   800 Kilometers

1.1
Morphological Regions of Northern Canada

ery are of great age because they were certainly in existence by the mid-Palaeozoic and possibly in the late Precambrian.

Evolution of the Shield Landscapes

Towards the close of the Precambrian the Canadian Shield was reduced to a vast region of low relief broken by occasional residual hill ranges. At least one of these, the Wellington arch in southern Victoria Island, has survived to the present after exhumation from later sediments. Endogenous forces produced on the Shield surface an undulating pattern of arches and domes separated by basins several hundred miles across. This wave form has continued to dominate the surface through a large part of Phanerozoic time.

Denudation has removed much of the Palaeozoic, carbonate rock cover from the Shield, although these rocks survive in the platform zone northwest and west of the Shield margin, and on the north side where they occupy troughs between the Boothia and Minto Shield arches. Within the Shield they are found in the Hudson, Moose (James), Foxe, and Ungava basins. The scenery on the carbonate rocks is characterized by plains, low plateaus, and cuestas, often with a felsenmeer surface. Broad areas, particularly of the inner basins, are covered by shallow seas; on the adjoining coasts conspicuous elevated strandlines and other evidence of the postglacial marine transgression are preserved.

The Palaeozoic sediments were removed by subaerial erosion, first from the crests of the Shield arches and domes, thus revealing the subpalaeozoic surface. This in turn was modified by erosion so that today its highest parts have either been destroyed, as in eastern Baffin Island, or have been much modified. Tentatively the main uplands of the interior Shield areas in the North, including the lake plateaus of Labrador–Quebec, and eastern Mackenzie–southwestern Keewatin may be interpreted as subpalaeozoic surfaces considerably modified by long periods of low-energy, subaerial denudation; the geomorphic evolution of these areas is almost certainly more complex, as is suggested by the example of central Keewatin.

Removal of the Palaeozoic cover has continued to the present time and, where exhumation dates from the Late Tertiary and Quaternary, the subpalaeozoic surface is little modified. The west shore of Ungava Bay, the Keewatin coast of Hudson Bay from Churchill to Roes Welcome Sound, most of Foxe Peninsula in southwest Baffin Island, and the south side of Queen Maud Gulf evolved in this way.

Other planation surfaces exist within the northern Shield, including broad rock benches many miles across, described from Baffin Island. It is clear that long periods of subaerial exposure led to deep weathering and in northern Canada, as elsewhere, much of the detail of today's Shield scenery results from late Tertiary and Quaternary removal of the weathered products.

The Shield has not been stable everywhere in the Phanerozoic. Regional crustal movements occurred particularly near the Baffin and Labrador coasts, culminating in the opening of Labrador Sea–Baffin Bay by continental drift, with accompanying vulcanism on the Cumberland Peninsula in the early Tertiary. Faulting in the Shield has been widespread and, although many faults were initiated in the Precambrian, activity continued through the Palaeozoic and in some cases probably much later. The straight coasts of Hudson Strait, Frobisher Bay, northeast Southampton Island, and many other places are probably the topographic expression of faults.

Evolution of the Borderlands
While these events were occurring in the Shield, the landscape of the borderlands was evolving. The Mackenzie and southern arctic islands basement platforms showed considerable crustal stability in late Mesozoic and Tertiary times and landscape evolution is explained primarily in terms of subaerial denudation of horizontally bedded sedimentary rocks, e.g. the elevated plain that survives today as the Barrow upland surface in parts of western Devon Island, northwest Baffin, Somerset, and eastern Prince of Wales islands at a height of 325–425 m (1100–1400 ft). The surface is disrupted by channels that separate the upland into the islands of the central archipelago. The straight coasts of many of the channels suggest that faulting was responsible, but it is not known if they are first-cycle graben, or whether a more complex evolution has occurred. It is recognized that the submerged channels at one time were modified by fluvial, and in the east, glacial processes.

Development of Drainage Patterns
Two ancient drainage systems existed in northern Canada. Many of the larger Shield rivers developed on the Palaeozoic sedimentary cover and in the early Tertiary may have extended from the rising eastern ranges of the Cordillera across the Shield to the Labrador Sea (Figure 1.2). Progressively this pattern was disrupted by expansion of the stripped Shield domes and by adjustment of the drainage to surviving sedimentary areas. The headwaters of the system were captured by the growth of the proto-

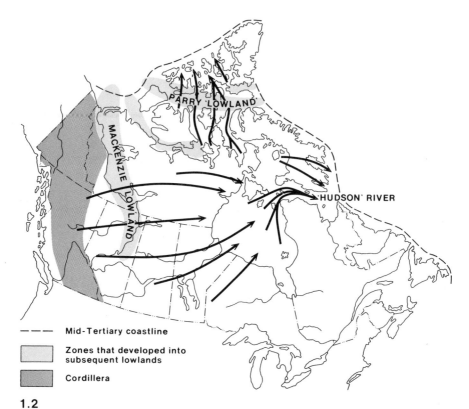

1.2

Hypothetical Tertiary Drainage of Northern Canada

Mackenzie between the Cordillera and the Shield, and today all the Hudson Bay rivers except the Saskatchewan have been beheaded. Although the Mackenzie provides a classic example of a subsequent continental river, in detail its course presents major problems of which the history of the delta and the origin of the antecedent (superimposed) section where it enters the Cordillera separating the Franklin from the Mackenzie mountains are probably the most difficult.

The drainage of the High Arctic in the pre-Archipelago period was primarily towards the Sverdrup Basin and was controlled in detail by fault zones. The pattern became disrupted during the formation of Parry Channel, which is suspected of having a tectonic origin, and probably by the sinking of the northwestern Arctic which was associated with the late Tertiary transgression of the 'Beaufort' Sea.

In the Tertiary the second-order landscape elements appear; in the sedimentary basins endogenetic forces continued to be important while in the Shield and on the platforms, although they were present, denudation had an important and probably dominant role. By the end of the Tertiary the first- and second-order landforms resembled those of today, except for the extent of the shallow continental seas. The detail of the landscape, the third-order elements, were, however, to experience major modifications in the Quaternary.

Northern Canada in the Quaternary

The existence of multiple Pleistocene glaciations in northern Canada is firmly established from the presence of interstadial and/or interglacial organic beds in the Hudson Bay Lowland, on Central Baffin Island, in the northwest arctic coastal plain, and on the western Queen Elizabeth Islands. At the close of the Sangamon interglacial, ice caps began to accumulate on the uplands that form the backbone of Baffin Island, in locations analogous to the present-day Barnes Ice Cap. As the climatic deterioration intensified, ice caps formed in northern Quebec–Labrador. After these ice caps had expanded sufficiently to modify the regional climates, snow fields developed rapidly and permanent ice engulfed all the Canadian North – east of the Cordillera and south of Parry Channel – to produce the Laurentide Ice Sheet. At the maximum of the Wisconsin glaciation the only ice-free areas were nunataks and one or more narrow coastal zones adjacent to Baffin Bay and Labrador Sea.

In the Northwest an independent Cordilleran ice sheet occupied northern British Columbia and southern Yukon; central Yukon remained free of ice probably because of aridity resulting from the topographic blocking of Pacific sources of moisture by the St Elias and Coast ranges, and the mountain barrier of the eastern Cordillera to the Laurentide Ice Sheet. A single, thin and probably immobile ice sheet, the Innuitian, appears to have covered the Queen Elizabeth Islands.

Waning of the Wisconsin glaciation first began in the North about 13,000 years ago. It was not until about 10,000 B.P. that an ice-free corridor appeared in the Northwest between the Cordillera and the Shield. At this time an ice-free zone along the Atlantic coast was less than 150 km (93 mi) wide. By 8000 B.P., Pleistocene ice had vanished from the Queen Elizabeth Islands and the northern Cordillera. In the next thousand years catastrophic changes in the Laurentide Ice Sheet occurred when the sea broke into Hudson Bay through Hudson Strait and the continental ice sheet disintegrated into smaller ice caps centred over interior Keewatin, northern Quebec, Baffin Island, and some of the smaller arctic peninsulas and islands. By 5500 B.P. the glacierized area of the Arctic was probably less than today.

The most conspicuous landscape changes produced by the ice were in areas of high relief that experienced mountain glaciation. The alpine landscape of east Baffin Island and northern Labrador with deep glacial trough valleys, cirques, pyramidical peaks, and fiords are as spectacular as any in the world. Changes in other mountains varied depending on the degree of glacierization; some northern mountains, notably the interior ranges of the Richardson Mountains escaped glaciation entirely. Mountains developed on crystalline and highly metamorphosed rocks as in eastern Ellesmere Island and the Ogilvie Mountains (Y.T.) show striking erosional glacial forms while others on sedimentary rocks, for example on Axel Heiberg Island, often show few glacial landforms and these rarely are strongly developed.

The lowlands between the western mountains and the northeastern highlands are dominated by depositional glacial landforms, but even here, especially on the northern islands and in the Mackenzie Lowland, glacial deposits may be totally absent. In contrast, extensive drift areas are preserved in the Shield on both sides of Hudson Bay and on eastern Victoria Island. The surface of these till plains has been patterned by the motion of the ice into drumlins and drumlinoid ridges that control the drainage and the local terrain. Fluvioglacial deposits are widely distributed particularly in the form of eskers, especially in Keewatin and eastern Mackenzie. Outwash deposits from the ice are of limited importance in the lowland areas covered by the Laurentide Ice Sheet, but in the Mackenzie Lowland and especially in the interior valleys of the Yukon they dominate the landscape at lower elevations. In the far north the direct morphological impact of the glaciation on the landscape has been so slight, excepting the mountains, that for a long time the evidence was thought inadequate to indicate glaciation.

Marine transgression flooded most coastal lowlands as the ice withdrew. Everywhere in northern coastal areas, except for the shores of the Beaufort Sea where the transgression reached less than 10 m (33 ft) above the present level, sediments and shoreline features have been elevated by crustal rebound. The transgression was most extreme in Keewatin where the sea extended 500 km (311 mi) westwards of the present shoreline. The highest, raised, postglacial marine features are on the east side of Hudson Bay where they reach nearly 275 m (900 ft). Rebound at the outer perimeter of the ice sheets was virtually complete before the ice had vanished from the interior zone. Emergence in the central parts of northern Canada is continuing and it has been perceptible in the Hudson Bay area over the past two centuries. The impact of the marine inundation on the landscape is most evident on thin-bedded sedimentary rock plains including the Palaeozoic limestone borderlands and the basalt low-lands around Coronation Gulf.

CONTEMPORARY PHYSICAL PROCESSES

The Atmosphere

High latitude results in a winter period of net radiation loss which lasts in the northern islands up to seven months. The Cordillera is a significant topographic element in the development of the climate as it effectively blocks off maritime Pacific air from the northlands, and for long periods, from the interior plateaus of the Yukon. The complementary effect is the absence of any considerable barrier to north–south movement of air masses in the central and eastern parts of the continent.

The surface circulation in the circumpolar regions in winter is dominated by a massive semi-permanent high pressure area corresponding to a heat sink and extending from a centre in northeast Siberia (1,035 mb) by a ridge across the Arctic Ocean to a smaller centre over the Mackenzie Lowland (1,023 mb). At this season the oceanic lows are over the north Atlantic and Pacific; from the former, a trough, corresponding to open water, extends into the Labrador Sea and Davis Strait. The day-to-day pressure patterns are more complex, but the overall result in northern Canada, east of the Cordillera, is a resultant air flow from the north which has originated in the Alaska–Yukon High, in northern Siberia, or in north Greenland. Invariably this air is intensely cold, temperatures of −50°C (−58°F) are common and may occasionally fall to −60°C (−76°F). Although wind conditions over the Queen Elizabeth Islands and the lower Mackenzie are generally quiet, the pressure gradient steepens towards the east coast and strong, persistent northwesterly winds, and the accompanying extreme wind chill, are among the chief characteristics of the central and eastern arctic and subarctic climate in winter.

Incursions of maritime air from the Pacific occasionally modify the extreme cold in the Yukon and Mackenzie Lowland and these areas often experience both the coldest and the highest winter temperatures in the Canadian North. Incursions of maritime polar air with easterly winds from the Atlantic occur at least once a winter in southern Baffin Island and more frequently in Quebec–Labrador. They are associated with deep stationary cyclonic lows over the Labrador Sea and rain commonly accompanies the relatively high temperatures.

Winter precipitation in the North usually results from frontal activity, but because of the low absolute humidities is generally light. The exception is close to the eastern seaboard where the incursion of tropical maritime air aloft associated with depressions is accompanied by heavy snowfalls over the Quebec–Labrador plateau; total winter snowfall in the easter Subarctic may exceed 300 cm (118 in.). A zone of low snowfall (50–100 cm; 20–39 in.) extends from the arctic islands into the eastern Mackenzie and Keewatin districts. Farther west there is a slight increase of snowfall in the Mackenzie Lowland and the intermontane interior of the Yukon resulting from the entry in the upper atmosphere of Pacific maritime air.

Towards the end of March the weather patterns begin to change and for a month in the northern Subarctic and for longer in the Arctic it is a period of increasing sunshine and calm weather, and in the west the first signs of spring as the air temperature begins to rise perceptibly. The threshold of spring, as measured by the mean air temperature rising above 0°C (32°F) is of great importance as thereafter snow disappears quickly. The date varies enormously. The earliest dates are in the southern Mackenzie Lowland where the threshold is normally reached in the third week of April. By 10 May all the Lowland except for the delta is above freezing point. Spring conditions also advance rapidly in the Yukon, but in the Arctic winter hangs on. Late May and early June is a period of striking climatic gradient from the western Subarctic, where it is already warm and plants are in flower, to the Barren Grounds, perhaps no more than 150 km (93 mi) away, which are still under snow. Early June sees the arrival of terrestrial spring with much of the lowland snow melting throughout the remainder of the Arctic although lakes may be ice-covered for another month. With continuous sunshine and low winter snowfall in the high Arctic, it is not unusual for the ground to be clear of snow in 80°N, while there is still a 50 per cent cover 1,200 km (746 mi) farther south.

Summer is also a season of contrasts although they are of a different nature from those of winter. The most marked change results from the replacement of a 'continental' surface of snow-covered sea ice in Hudson Bay, Foxe Basin and over the Archipelago by water, albeit with a surface temperature close to 0°C (32°F). The pressure field also undergoes rapid change with the disappearance of the high pressure systems, except for the survival of a ridge over the Pacific sector of the Arctic Ocean, and the weakening of the Aleutian and Icelandic lows. The summer mean pressure map shows a feeble pressure pattern and the resultant mean air flow is weak. Over the islands the wind continues to be from the north and northwest, but south of the arctic front, which has a mean position at this season corresponding closely to the treeline, winds are from the west.

The day-to-day pressure pattern in summer commonly consists of a succession of shallow disturbances passing eastwards across the Barren Grounds and the southern arctic islands. The summer cyclones resemble those of mid-latitudes, with warm, humid air drawn in on the southern flank. In the northwest, this results in warm, unstable showery weather, frequently accompanied by thunderstorms. However, in the central and eastern districts a shallow cold layer usually persists at the surface and rain falling through it from above produces considerable low cloud and fog. The disturbances have a tendency to be blocked over southern Baffin Bay and Hudson Strait and long periods of cold, cloudy, damp weather in the eastern Canadian Arctic are associated with this situation.

In some years summer anticyclones become established in the North, particularly over the western Arctic, and in these circumstances several weeks of warm, dry, cloudless weather, with unbroken sunshine, may develop. Summer temperatures rarely exceed 15°C (59°F) in eastern coastal and northern areas where the presence of the cold sea can rarely be forgotten climatically for more than a few hours, although at inland sites in the eastern Subarctic annual maxima of 24–26°C (75–79°F) are not unknown. There are significant regional differences in summer between the Mackenzie Lowland and interior Yukon when the mean for July reaches nearly 15°C (59°F) almost to the Arctic Ocean, and the damp, cloudy, central and eastern northlands, where, although precipitation is no greater than in the west, its longer duration, the lower temperatures, and heavy cloud give the impression of much wetter conditions.

The fall begins in late August in the high Arctic and advances at a uniform rate until by mid to late September it has arrived on the shores of southern Hudson Bay. It is a period of storminess, broken by occasional calm spells and dropping temperatures. By late October winter has set in with a continuous snow cover throughout the North.

Local deviations are often more important than regional variations. The cold summer seas produce shallow inversions that affect coastal districts and local differences in the mountain zones, particularly winter temperature inversions and relatively warm valley winds in summer, are equally striking. Any possibility of climatic change in the North is clearly of considerable significance. The postglacial, prehistoric climatic optimum was reached in the North 6000 years ago, about the time the last Pleistocene ice sheet vanished. A deterioration of climate followed before a second warm phase developed about a thousand years ago. Renewed deterioration culminated in glacier advances in the eighteenth and nineteenth centuries which have left prominent terminal moraines. In the present century and especially since 1930 there has been some climatic amelioration. It is not known whether the reversal of temperature trends observed elsewhere in the northern hemisphere since 1940 has also occurred in northern Canada.

The Air/Ground Interface – Contemporary Glaciation

Less than 5 per cent of the Canadian Arctic is covered with glacier ice and the distribution is so restricted that probably two-thirds of the Eskimo population has never seen a glacier. The distribution of glaciers is closely linked with altitude. In the Canadian North, with few exceptions, elevations above 600 m (1969 ft) are restricted to the Cordillera and the eastern highland rim; both upland regions support glaciers, but in the lowland zone between there is none.

Permanent land ice in the east is confined to the arctic islands except for cirque glaciers of the Torngat Mountains of northern Labrador. North of Cumberland Sound on Baffin Island permanent ice is significant, but with the exception of the Barnes ice cap in the centre of Baffin Island is confined to a 100 km (328 ft)-wide, coastal belt dissected by numerous fiords. The glacierized area increases north of Parry Channel where one-third of Ellesmere and Axel Heiberg islands are covered with ice. In the northeast there are a dozen ice caps with areas greater than 3000 km² (1158 sq mi). Some ice caps including the Barnes and east Devon are situated on plateaus, others such as the Penny and Bylot are highland ice which bury partly or wholly underlying mountains.

West of the main zone of arctic ice, small glaciers exist on Meighen and Melville islands. The former has a dome-shaped, oval ice cap with a summit under 275 m (902 ft), and is unique in the Canadian Arctic because of its low altitude. Its greatest thickness is under 120 m (394 ft) and there is no significant flow. Five hundred kilometres (300 mi) to the southwest on Melville Island, four small ice caps, the only glaciers in the western Arctic, survive above 1000 m (3281 ft).

In the interior and eastern ranges of the Cordillera, low precipitation and relatively high summer temperatures preclude all but a few glaciers from the eastern Yukon and the bordering Mackenzie mountains. In contrast, in the St Elias Range a combination of altitude and the proximity of the Pacific Ocean produces immense ice fields.

Ice in the Ground – Permafrost

Investigations in northern Canada in the past two decades have emphasized that perennially frozen ground is a significant parameter in the northern physical and biological environmental systems. By definition, permafrost is the thermal condition existing in earth materials that remain below 0°C (32°F) for several years. Nearly a quarter of Canada is under-

1.3

Distribution of Continuous and Discontinuous Permafrost in Canada

lain by continuous permafrost, and discontinuous permafrost is found in an additional quarter of the country. Permafrost develops when the radiative and conductive energy balance at the surface, plus heat transfer from the interior of the earth, contributes to an equilibrium condition below 0°C (32°F). Empirically it has been found that, when the mean annual air temperature falls below −7°C (+19°F), continuous permafrost is commonly present; exceptions are beneath the sea and large freshwater bodies, both lakes and rivers. A good correlation exists between the treeline and the southern limit of the continuous permafrost as the position of the treeline integrates many of the parameters that are involved in the distribution of permafrost. (The exception of northern Quebec is apparently influenced by the heavy snowfall in the area.)

All the Canadian arctic islands, the Barren Grounds west of Hudson Bay, and a small area in far northern Quebec are underlaid by continuous permafrost. On the islands the permafrost reaches a depth in excess of

500 m (1640 ft), while on the mainland the deepest permafrost may be about 400 m (1312½ ft) in the Pleistocene Mackenzie delta. Towards the southern edge of the continuous zone the thickness of permafrost decreases and is generally 40–60 m (131–197 ft).

The transition zone in which permafrost occurs discontinuously in some, but not in all localities, is in many ways economically more significant than the zone of continuous permafrost. This belt is nearly 500 km (311 mi) wide south of James Bay, but broadens to the east and west to about twice this width. In the discontinuous zone, particularly near the southern limit, permafrost is restricted to north-facing slopes, treeless ridges which are blown clear of snow in the winter, and lowlands where poor drainage has led to the development of organic soils. There are indications that fossil permafrost may be widespread in the discontinuous zone and reach thicknesses in excess of 100 m (328 ft) although it is permanently separated from the winter cold wave by a ground layer above freezing point.

In northern Canada, perennial ice in addition to occurring on the land as glaciers and on the sea as shelf ice is also found in the ground. Massive ground ice is preserved along the Yukon coasts, in the present and Pleistocene Mackenzie deltas, around the shores of Amundsen Gulf, on Banks Island, and in the Parry and Sverdrup islands. Layers of ice over 30 m (98 ft) thick have been reported. The ice is exposed beneath silt and organic cappings in seacliffs and along the banks of streams where it contributes to rapid retreat and cliff slumping. In the Sverdrup Islands, parts of the lowlands are underlain by ice, and stream channel growth is frequently dominated by exposure and melting of ground ice.

Other forms of ground ice are widely distributed as ground moisture but where a permafrost condition prevails will normally be frozen, e.g. as a coating on rock particles or as hairline, vein, wedge, or lens ice. The largest quantities of ground ice normally occur in silts. In Canada these are widely distributed around the Beaufort Sea, and in the Sverdrup Basin, the lower Mackenzie Valley and the valleys and lowlands of central and north Yukon. The soils of the central and eastern Arctic, as well as most parts of the Subarctic rarely contain ground ice on the same scale as in the northwest, although it may be locally significant.

Irregular accumulation of ground ice in wedges is associated with tundra fissure polygons, and in 'blisters' of ice, with pingos. The latter are mounds and low conical hills, which may attain 45 m (148 ft) in height. One variety is found in the Pleistocene Mackenzie delta where over 1400 have been recognized; they commonly develop in the floors of shallow lakes. Several hundred of a second type of pingo located on the lower slopes and floors of valleys have been identified in the Pleistocene unglaciated zone of central Yukon.

Thermokarst, the uneven settling of the ground, develops where ground ice thaws and the moisture can drain away, the normal case in discontinuous permafrost. Unlike Alaska and Siberia, this type of thermokarst has not been widely reported from northern Canada. In other circumstances lake basins develop when ground ice thaws. If the basin expands by wave erosion of ice and silts around the shores, a characteristic lake shape results depending on the wind direction. When there is a dominant wind direction, elongated (oriented) lakes such as occur in the Old Crow Plain (Y.T.) and the Tuktoyaktuk Peninsula, are formed. When the wind direction is more evenly distributed, circular lakes of the type found on the Great Plain of the Koukdjuak, west central Baffin Island, are produced.

Above the permafrost table, ground ice is an annual phenomenon. It plays an important part in seasonal ground heaving and in the retention and accumulation of moisture near the surface. When it thaws during the early part of the summer, it is a major contributor to solifluction and other forms of mass movement.

Geomorphic Processes and Microlandforms

The landscapes of northern Canada are being modified today by periglacial and other geomorphic processes, though their effectiveness varies over the area. Weathering processes, especially frost shattering, are active in the periglacial environment, and weathering on Palaeozoic limestones, dolomites, and sandstones has been extremely rapid as may be seen in exposure on Cornwallis, west Devon, and other arctic islands. In contrast, rapid weathering on crystalline igneous rocks has been restricted generally to glacially overdeepened valleys.

The most widely recognized process of mass movement in the Arctic and the treeless localities of the Subarctic is solifluction. Induced by frost movement and flow associated with high moisture content, solifluction displaces the weathered mantle downslope either in discrete tongues or in sheets. The annual movement varies depending on moisture availability, soil particle size, and degree of slope, but is commonly 2–5 cm (0.2–2.0 in). Solifluction is probably active in all parts of the Canadian Arctic except the flattest plains; its incidence varies widely and may attain a maximum as an overall areal phenomenon on Banks Island and in the Sverdrup and Parry islands. In the Subarctic, solifluction is common in the mountains of central and northern Yukon, but elsewhere it is confined to hillslopes from which trees are absent, or other special localities.

Other periglacial forms of mass movement show regional distributions.

In this category are the rock glaciers of the northern Cordillera, and particularly the St Elias Range, the earth and mudflows of the northwestern lowlands, both on the mainland and the islands, and the rock streams on the valley floors of the northeastern Shield.

Microscale movements of the soil are responsible for much of the patterned ground that is observed in northern areas. Morphologically there are three major groups of patterned ground in northern Canada. One group consists of polygonal patterns varying in scale from several centimetres in width to a hundred metres (328 ft) and more that are formed by the intersection of cracks and fissures; e.g. large ice-wedge polygons are most representative of the silt plains of the western Arctic mainland and islands.

A second large group of features includes mounds, low domes and hollows, and mud circles, all more or less distributed in a regular pattern that results in many cases from movement associated with hydrostatic pressure developed in the subsurface by freezing; a third group comprises the patterns produced by sorting, in which fines are concentrated in one area, normally the centre of a circle or polygon and the larger particles form the perimeter. In practice much patterned ground is polygenetic and patterns derived from different processes are commonly superimposed.

Northern Soils

Soil movements that lead to patterned ground also effect the development of soil horizons, which because of soil mobility and limited biochemical action are generally youthful. As might be expected, the more mature soils are found in the Subarctic where the summers are warmer, and particularly in the northwest. In the valley floors of the Yukon and areas of restricted drainage in the Mackenzie Lowland, organic soils and dark grey gleisolic soils predominate. Similar soils are found at ill-drained sites in the central and eastern Subarctic and particularly in the Hudson Bay Lowland; where the drainage is better, a developmental sequence of profiles has been observed. Mineral soils containing no weathering (regosols) are found at many sites; at a slightly later stage, weathering in the upper horizon leads to the development of brown wooded soils which are widely distributed on elevated terrains in the Mackenzie Lowland. At a still later stage elluvial and illuvial horizons are differentiated to produce gray wooded and finally shallow podzol soils.

North of the treeline there are considerable differences. Polar desert soils with little organic matters and ephemeral salt crusts predominate in the islands north of Parry Channel. On the mainland and especially in the western Arctic the most widespread group is the intrazonal tundra soils. In these soils frost churning is important and gleization occurs near the surface where a blue-gray horizon is commonly speckled with humus and shows yellow-brown mottling. Soil subgroups may be differentiated between the better drained upland tundra soils and the meadow tundra soils. At many sites organic material has been incorporated into the horizons, including those that are now permanently frozen. Organic matter decomposes extremely slowly, and at poorly drained sites where there is little runoff and the permafrost table is close to the surface, bog soils are characteristic.

Arctic brown soils are found at some sites with effective drainage, especially close to the treeline and where the vegetation is shrub or heath tundra. They have been reported from numerous localities west of Hudson Bay, and from Prince Patrick, Banks and north Baffin islands where they develop when there is a deep active layer. The colour is a product of iron weathering from the parent material along with humus. Many southern arctic soils show evidence of podzolization and west of Hudson Bay podzol-like soils have been recorded. However, it is believed that some of these soils may be fossil, particularly a broad zone that has been mapped south of Dubawnt Lake.

Surface Water

The hydrology of the arctic environment has not been adequately studied. Arctic rivers, in common with streams in practically all parts of Canada, increase in flow as the snow cover melts in spring. There is no stream flow in medium and small arctic basins in winter. Flow commences in late May or June and rises abruptly to peak discharge within one or two weeks and decreases almost as rapidly to a low stage for the balance of the summer. It is not unusual for 80 per cent of the annual runoff to occur in less than 3 per cent of the year. Large rivers show a similar flow pattern although the variation is not as great. The maximum monthly flow of Back River is about twenty times the minimum flow, the Yukon River about ten times, while on the lower Mackenzie and its major tributaries the ratio is about five times, a figure somewhat higher than is typical in southern Canada. Excluding the eastern seaboard, the annual runoff throughout arctic Canada is under 15 cm (6 in.) or about half the average for the country, and on the arctic islands is less than 10 cm (4 in.). In the Subarctic there is a conspicuous difference between relatively low annual runoff in the west and in northern Quebec–Labrador, where it exceeds 50 cm (20 in.) over the greater part of the peninsula.

Vegetation

The vegetation of northern Canada is dominated by several types of tundra and polar deserts beyond the treeline, and by woodland south of it. The treeline cannot be defined precisely in the mountains of the Yukon since it is altitude dependent. East of the Cordillera the line extends from the Mackenzie Delta across the Northwest Territories and northern Manitoba to the vicinity of Hudson Bay near Churchill and then skirts the southern shores of the bay to James Bay. On the east side of Hudson Bay the boundary runs from the coast north of Great Whale River across the peninsula to the vicinity of Fort Chimo and from there to Labrador. The depression of the treeline in two areas south of 55° N by the cold waters of Hudson Bay and the Labrador Current places it farther south than any other coastal locality in the Northern Hemisphere. Along many rivers, including the Horton and Coppermine in the west and the Koksoak in Quebec, the treeline projects northwards into the Barren Grounds. The actual limit is influenced by many factors including summer temperatures, soil moisture, depth of snow cover, and permafrost, parameters which are themselves semi-dependent.

North of the treeline tundra, vegetation often appears remarkably uniform. However, in detail there is considerable variety and several major plant associations may be differentiated. The harshest environments such as occur at high elevations in all parts of the Arctic and on felsenmeer in the lowlands are responsible for *polar deserts*. In high arctic deserts vegetation may be completely absent except for crustaceous lichens; farther south many vascular plants occur as isolated individual species frequently growing as tussocks, and for a short period in summer even the desert is covered with flowers, especially in the more sheltered areas.

The remaining four arctic plant associations are varieties of tundra in which there is a continuous or virtually continuous vegetation cover. Under the driest conditions such as develop on outwash sands, river terraces, and sandy tills, *lichen-moss tundra* is the characteristic association; species of lichens, notably reindeer moss (*Cladonia*) are common and where the precipitation is high, especially in northern Quebec, they may form a dense continuous 'blanket' on the ground. Geographically, lichen-moss tundra is a phenomenon of the middle and parts of the southern Arctic; in the warmer areas and particularly in southern Keewatin and eastern Mackenzie districts it grades into heath tundra in which berry plants (*Empetrum nigrum, Vaccinium uliginosum*) are numerous.

In contrast to lichen-moss and heath tundras are the *wet tundras*, which develop in poorly drained habitats, generally on fine-grained soils in which ground ice is preserved. Wet tundra is found in all parts of arctic Canada although it decreases towards the pole. It forms a dense vegetation cover with grasses and damp-loving sedges (*Carex, Eriophorum*). In the south,

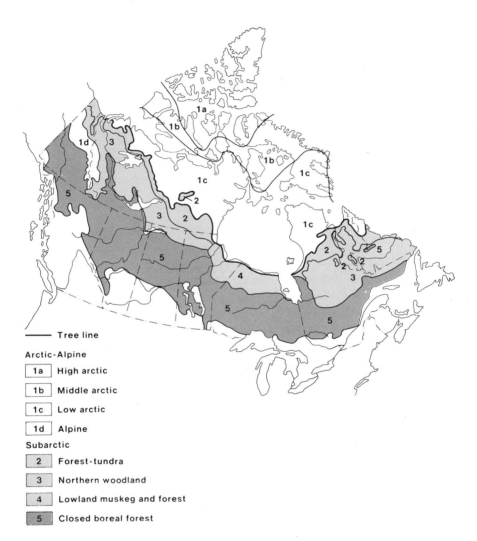

Tree line

Arctic-Alpine

1a	High arctic
1b	Middle arctic
1c	Low arctic
1d	Alpine

Subarctic

2	Forest-tundra
3	Northern woodland
4	Lowland muskeg and forest
5	Closed boreal forest

1.4
Vegetation of Arctic and Subarctic Canada

shrubs are important, particularly ground birch and Labrador Tea (*Ledum decumbens*). The most luxuriant southern tundra is the *bush* or *scrub tundra*. In Canada it reaches its finest development in the western Arctic in the sheltered valleys on the south side of Amundsen and Coronation gulfs. The dominant bushes are willows and occasionally alders, and there is frequently dense herbaceous undergrowth. On south-facing slopes, where snow provides protection from winter winds and where there is an adequate water supply during the summer, bushes may form dense woods with individual shrubs attaining 3 m (10 ft) or more in height. In the eastern Arctic similar scrub areas occur in protected valleys on both sides of Hudson Strait, but they are not common. In somewhat less-favoured areas near the treeline, willow and birch scrub thickets grow in open localities and individual bushes are 0.5–1.0 m (1.6–3 ft) high. The microclimate and fauna in the scrub zones is often very different from that of the adjacent tundra. In winter the scrub is practically buried by snow, but in summer it provides sheltered areas which provide cover for birds and small animals (tree sparrow, *Spizella arborea*, etc.) that are typical of the subarctic woodlands at this season.

The most northerly trees in Canada close to the treeline are generally white or black spruce (*Picea glauca, Picea mariana*) although locally in Quebec–Labrador it is larch (*Larix laricina*). Immediately south of the regional treeline, tundra continues to be areally dominant. At first, islands or strips of trees are restricted to sheltered areas. This constitutes the forest–tundra zone which typically varies in width from 50 km (31 mi) in western Canada to over 150 km (93 mi) in parts of northern Labrador–Ungava. Within the forest–tundra, environments representative of the Arctic occur, in which there is deep permafrost, and in winter strong blowing snow and serious problems of exposure for animals and plants; they alternate with the forest environment in which the snow is deep and less well-packed and permafrost may be absent.

South of the forest–tundra is the open parkland of the northern boreal forest. It reaches its finest development east of Hudson Bay, where the woodland is dominated by widely separated Candelabra spruce standing on a deep lichen floor. Where the drainage is less effective, particularly southwest of Hudson Bay, there is a wet or muskeg type, northern forest in which black spruce and larch are characteristic trees and the ground is covered with sphagnum moss and shrubs; string bogs are widely distributed and palsen are numerous.

Air/Sea Interface

Two major oceanic circulations affect Canada's northern seas. In the Arctic Ocean, off the northwest coast, the circulation is clockwise at about 5 cm (2 in.) sec^{-1} over the continental shelf, although rarely measurable inshore. The current carries pack ice and occasionally ice islands along the nothwest coast of Canada and extremely heavy, old ice is forced against the outermost islands. At depth a reverse current of intermediate water of Atlantic origin probably exists, but its presence is not obvious on the surface. Off the east coast, a south-flowing current, known as the Canada current in Baffin Bay and the Labrador current in the Labrador Sea, is a stream of arctic water rather less than 325 km (202 mi) wide that originates in northern Baffin Bay and carries masses of ice and cold water as far south as Newfoundland.

In the seas between the two major circulations are smaller and often local currents. There is believed to be a drift of surface water from the Arctic Ocean through the Queen Elizabeth Islands in a southerly and southeasterly direction which reinforces the Canada current. In the southern archipelago currents are small, although an influx of water along the north shore of the mainland eastwards from Amudsen Gulf has been observed. The circulation in Hudson Bay is anticlockwise with an inflow from the north side of Hudson Strait and Foxe Channel and an outflow between Coats Island and northwest Quebec. In Hudson Strait, inflow from Davis Strait is on the north side and outflow on the south side.

Between the islands and in Hudson Bay the water masses are believed to be homogeneous with uniform arctic characteristics to the bottom. In Baffin Bay three water masses have been recognized: a surface layer resulting from mixing of water from several sources; an intermediate warmer layer at depths of 200 to 1,000 m (656–3281 ft); and beneath this a second cold water mass.

With the exception of icebergs in the Canada/Labrador current and ice islands, virtually all sea ice in Canadian northern waters is annual; exceptions are in the northwest where perennial ice may be driven inshore and into M'Clure Strait: and between the Sverdrup Islands where fast ice may survive from one year to the next. Elsewhere, September is the month of minimum sea ice. By late August new ice has already begun to form in far northern waters and freezing extends, until by late October ice occurs inshore in all seas when the weather is calm. A continuous ice cover is, however, slow in becoming established since storms in the late fall break up the ice and drive it out into the open sea as pack. By early December, in an average year, the enclosed seas in the archipelago are ice-covered and by the end of the year Hudson Bay has a continuous sheet of ice except for local leads.

Between January and early April the only open waters in the Canadian North are leads, formed where tidals currents are strong, e.g. on the north side of Hudson Strait, or where there are practically continuous off-shore winds, as along the south coast of Southampton Island. In north Baffin Bay open water may persist throughout the winter owing to a combination of winds which drive the pack south and upwelling of warmer subsurface waters.

Inshore ice patterns vary greatly in the North. In general, in the eastern Arctic where the tidal range is from 3–15 m (10–49 ft), stormy conditions prevail in winter and the seas are comparatively open, there is generally extremely rough ice inshore, while offshore the ice is broken and drifts in large floes. In contrast, in the calmer western and central Arctic where the tidal range is under 2 m (7 ft), smooth unbroken ice, except in the Arctic Ocean, is commonplace.

REGIONAL PHYSICAL ENVIRONMENTS

The differences between the physical conditions prevailing in several areas of northern Canada may be shown by a map of regionalization partly subjective, as perceived by indigenous peoples and European-Canadians, and partly objective based on physical parameters. A fundamental threefold division may be recognized between the high mountains – the Cordillera, the Subarctic, and the Arctic, with significant subdivisions within the latter two regions.

The characteristic of the northern Cordillera in terms of physical environment is the variation caused primarily by altitudinal differences: deep, but broad, terrace-filled, forested valleys contrast with the barren mountain and plateau summits. The climate shows local variety because of topography and also between the high snow-fall, glacier-covered ranges of the Pacific rim, and the subhumid mountains of the north.

Within the Subarctic the Mackenzie Lowland is perceived by most people as environmentally the most attractive region for settlement principally because of its warm summers and the relatively calm low-snow winters. It is in many ways a northern extension of the Interior Plains. The climate is subhumid, permafrost is discontinuous, and the woodlands tend to be open and broken up. To the east, the Western Shield is in winter transitional to the windier east; the psysiological cold is greater than in the Mackenzie Lowland and spring and summer are noticeably cooler. Trees in the northern part are scattered in clumps separated by broad tundra zones; in the south the woods are continuous except in areas of rock outcrops.

The Hudson Bay Lowland shares a similarity with the Mackenzie region in the underlying sedimentary rocks, and outcrops are few. This region is characterized by vast numbers of shallow lakes, muskeg and marsh in the badly drained areas, and stunted black spruce woods elsewhere. The Eastern Shield in northern Quebec–Labrador differs from the Western Shield in the stormier year-round weather and particularly in the long snowy winters. Annual runoff is significantly higher than elsewhere in

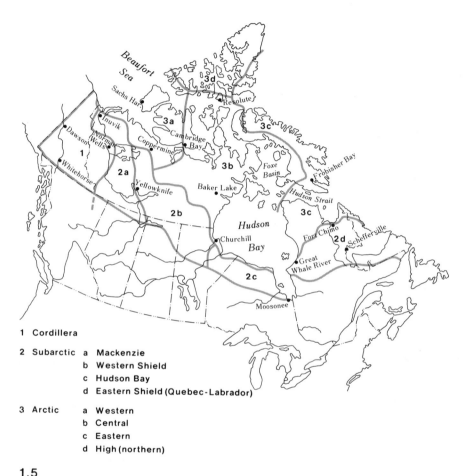

1 Cordillera

2 Subarctic   a Mackenzie
              b Western Shield
              c Hudson Bay
              d Eastern Shield (Quebec-Labrador)

3 Arctic   a Western
              b Central
              c Eastern
              d High (northern)

1.5
Physical Regions of Northern Canada

the Subarctic and the moist conditions are reflected in the fine development of the lichen floor in the woodlands.

Within the Arctic, the Western Section is the arctic continuation of the
Mackenzie Lowland. It is a region of low relief, silt-covered, ground ice-
rich terrains. Wet tundra overlying peat dominates much of the area. To
the east, the Central Section is characterized by the long, intensely cold
and windy winters. Containing most of the continental barren grounds and
the peninsulas that extend northwards, it includes considerable contrasts
between the Shield and the limestone areas. The Eastern Section is the

snowy part of the Arctic and in it are numerous glaciers. Open water is rarely far off shore even in late winter and occasional warm winter spells are not uncommon. The summer, however, is a period of storms, low cloud, and only moderate temperatures.

Finally at the far pole of the environmental spectrum is the High Arctic with long dark winters and relatively quiet conditions. The summer weather is variable, as might be expected close to high mountains. Much of the area is inaccessible from the sea because of ice conditions; parts of it are desert, with little vegetation and alluvial forms and ephemeral drainage more typical of hot deserts. It is the least known part of the North and the region that lacks true settlements. In its variey, is aridity, and its glaciers, and above all its potential for petroleum development, it is perhaps the most fascinating of all the regions of northern Canada.

2 L'écoumène du Nord canadien

LOUIS-EDMOND HAMELIN

Pour laisser entrevoir les éclairages, le contenu et les contours du sujet, rappelons d'abord les élements essentiels remués par le mot écoumène cette partie la plus géographique de l'espace. D'après Milton Santos, la surface terrestre en référence à l'homme-habitant 'est un espace réel, global, marqué par des activités chargées d'histoire et pénétré de modernité, un espace défini par des structures et parcouru par des flux, un espace où des décisions locales s'anastomosent avec des décisions lointaines, un espace qui est l'assiette d'un équilibre entre tous ces facteurs.' Cette présentation analytique correspond assez bien à une définition structurelle et génétique de l'écoumène; cependant, pour en arriver à saisir l'espace habité dans sa totalité, il faudrait ajouter à la description précédente la différenciation précisément spatiale de emprises humaines. D'une manière simple, l'écoumène, c'est l'espace terrestre vu quant à des faits d'habitation, d'exploitation, d'organisation et de culture. Bref, l'écoumène qui prend racine dans des états écologiques devient une combinaison complexe à incidences démographique, économique, culturelle, voire même subjective. Dans les recherches, l'écoumène doit alors occuper un très large domaine puisqu'il peut être considéré à la fois comme moteur et résidu de l'implantation des hommes. L'importance de cet espace répond à la préoccupation très géographique d'étudier dans leur mobilité spatiale des équilibres dynamiques à incidence humaine. Au cours de l'évolution de l'humanité, l'espace s'est présenté comme une variable à la fois dépendante et peu élastique. Il en fut ainsi dans le Nord canadien.

En fait, le texte qui suit va se tenir en retrait de cette conception totale de l'espace humain. Pour éviter des répétitions, les aspects, écologie, population et politique qui font l'objet d'autres chapitres de ce livre ne seront pas traités. La matière qui nous reste est toutefois abondant et nous la présenterons d'après une perspective historique, dans une préoccupation à la fois thématique et régionale et suivant une organisation structurelle.

Enfin, il ne s'agit pas de présenter systématiquement une série d'écoumènes spécialisés, par exemple l'ancien domaine de la Compagnie de la

Baie d'Hudson, la répartition des populations, les aires linguistiques, les diocèses, la prospection pétrolière, les réserves amérindiennes, les frontières politiques, l'espace couvert par les télécommunications ... Cet article qui n'est pas conçu pour remplacer un atlas s'en tiendra à des commentaires généraux.

ELEMENTS THEMATIQUES DE L'ECOUMENE DU CANADA SEPTENTRIONAL

Limites méridionales du Nord canadien

L'établissement d'une frontière sud pour la région nordique constitue le premier problème à résoudre. Les difficultés de la question expliquent peut-être le peu d'attention que cet aspect a reçu jusqu'à un passé très récent. Non qu'il n'existe pas de limites thématiques du Nord; au contraire, celles-ci sont nombreuses et elles comprennent au moins le cercle arctique, le 60è degré de latitude pour les Territoires-du-Nord-Ouest, le 52è pour le Québec, l'isotherme de 10°C (50°F) en juillet, l'isoligne subarctique pour les mois d'été, les frontières du permafrost continu et discontinu, le limbe taïga-toundra, la limite nord des activités agricoles, le domaine esquimau. L'on n'évitera pas de remarquer que ces critères ont la plupart du temps été considérés séparément; en conséquence, la ligne sud de la toundra, même si le facteur végétal a subi l'influence de plusieurs éléments correspond beaucoup plus à une frontière spécialisée, disons botanique, qu'à une délimitation globalement géographique; le facteur végétal ne s'applique pas aux régions hydrographiques – et l'Hudsonie crée une vaste coupure dans les terres canadiennes – et il dit peu de choses du poids du plénihiver, du pergélisol à plafond bas, de l'accessibilité de la région, du nombre d'habitants, de l'exploitation de ressources minières. La toundra comme chacun des autres critères singuliers, en fournissant une limite particulière du Nord relève de l'analyse séparatoire des choses, non d'une conception globale. Or, l'écoumène reflète justement des structurations d'équilibre; il est donc mal logé dan des domaines définis par les spécialistes d'une seule chose. De plus, la pluralité de limites particulières, plus ou moins parallèles, ne crée pas pour autant une frontière méridonale intégrée du Nord.

Le besoin nous a poussés à conceptualiser une méthode de calcul à laquelle nous renvoyons le lecteur; elle peut conduire à l'établissement d'un tel limbe global (Hamelin 1968). L'indice est basé sur dix facteurs et il exprime la nordicité en une certaine quantité de VAPO. L'isoligne de 200 VAPO permet de localiser les limites du Nord et partant celles de l'écoumène.

En 1970, cette frontière, large de 50 kilomètres (31 mi) environ, recouvre localement la limite méridonale du subarctique thermique qui se trouve généralement plus au sud. Au Canada, la frange du monde nordique suit la partie orientale de la Côte-Nord du Saint-Laurent, évite l'Abitibi, se maintient de là jusqu'au Manitoba près du 50è degré de latitude, touche au secteur médian de la Rivière de la Paix, atteint le Sud-Est de l'Alaska et se redresse vers le Nord-Ouest en longeant les chaînes côtières de la Colombie septentrionale. Cette ligne géographique majeure place plus de 70 pour cent du territoire canadien à l'intérieur des pays froids de latitude. En somme, le Nord comprend le Yukon, les Territoires-du-Nord-Ouest et la partie septentrionale de sept provinces. Dans cette vaste étendue nordique, vit à peine un quart de million de Canadiens.

Nord et Ecoumène
Au préalable, une autre question se pose. L'écoumène s'étend-il à la grandeur du Nord? Evidemment, la réponse tient à la définition même des termes. Nous considérons l'ensemble du Nord canadien comme écouméné, quitte à reconnaître qu'il l'est d'une manière extensive ou passive. Cette façon de voir ne doit pas surprendre. Le Nord est en train d'entrer dans les préoccupations canadiennes. L'opinion du professeur W.L. Morton (1970): 'The convention of Canadian life is to ignore the North,' vaut surtout pour l'historiographie. Le centenaire en 1967 a, dans son symbole officiel, consacré au Nord son triangle de tête. Certains observateurs se basant sur les faits que le Canada a été totalement photographié et qu'il est militairement surveillé prétendront qu'il est entièrement écouméné. Peu d'espaces ont été et sont compètement évités par les explorateurs, les Indigènes, les prospecteurs, les trappeurs, les pêcheurs, les réseaux de fréquence, les lignes séismiques et le vols aériens (commerciaux et militaires). Et il ne faudrait pas oublier l'exploitation prochaine et massive du pétrole et du gaz. A vrai dire, les môles ou secteurs pratiquement délaissés se rattachent davantage à un écoumène négatif qu'à un non-écoumène. La préoccupation pratiquement nouvelle de l'aspect propriété porte aussi toute son importance. L'affaire du *Manhattan* et la loi fédérale de 1970 qui établit une ceinture de protection autour de l'archipel arctique définissent nettement le territoire nordique du Canada par rapport à l'homme, c'est-à-dire aux Canadiens. N'y trouve-t-on pas là le sens fondamental du mot écoumène? En ce qui concerne le Nord, parallèlement au Gouvernement fédéral qui tend à appliquer une politique 'nationale' le principal gouvernement nordique provincial, celui du Québec, développe lui aussi une attitude émotive. L'argument à l'effet que le Nord constitue un territoire pratiquement vide d'habitants, à preuve les cartes presque sans cho-

ronymes ne vaut guère; dans bien des cas, il existe des milliers de noms utilisés par les Indigènes de passage; le fait que les Euro-canadiens n'ont pas recueilli ces termes contribue certes à la décertification apparente, mais il ne la prouve pas. En conséquence, la géographie humaine s'intéresse donc à tout l'espace nordique du Canada.

Vastitude

Vu ainsi, le Nord canadien est d'abord caractérisé par la vastitude, suivant un néologisme que Gabrielle Roy a appliqué à l'Alsama.[1] Dans le passé, pleine reconnaissance de cette immensité n'a pas été faite. En effet, de tradition, le Canada était un pays de terre et d'eau douce; le trait pourtant si typiquement canadien de la profonde pénétration des eaux marines est longtemps demeuré en dehors de la conscience nationale, peut-être par suite des déceptions dépétées causées par la non-commercialisation du Passage du Nord-Ouest. Comme le Gouvernement canadien entend désormais exercer sa juridiction sur les eaux salées et saumâtres des nappes subarctiques et arctiques, l'on devrait ajouter aux statistiques terrestres officielles, la superficie des eaux marines en voie de canadianisation; l'espace nordique du Canada gagnerait ainsi en juridiction, si jamais en propriété, plus d'un million de km carrés. Ainsi à lui seul le Nord canadien (terres et toutes eaux) occuperait un espace comparable à celui de l'ensemble des Etats-Unis. Même, en ne considérant que l'aspect terrestre, la superficie des Territoires-du-Nord-Ouest seulement fait plus du double de celle de l'Alaska.

Géographiquement, toute vastitude exprime à la fois des espoirs et des misères. Dans l'esprit des travaux de A. Siegfried, l'espace canadien non favorable à une économie modern était considére 'non utile'; du moins, il n'aurait pas été réclamé au compte de l'espace vital. Cette conception a fait place à une autre. Les vastes pays ont pris conscience de la valeur potentielle de leurs réserves en étendue. L'espace en abondance peut être un grenier de matières premières, un précieux réservoir d'eau douce pour les Etats-Unis bientôt assoiffés, un môle refuge pour des expériences scientifiques, une marche militaire (*Dew Line*), un axe de navigation sous-glacielle, une aire pour des communautés culturelles quasi uniques au monde (Esquimaux). Evidemment, les territories de chasse de l'île de

---

1 Alsama, néologisme (Hamelin 1966) destiné à remplacer les désignations géographiquement inexactes de 'Prairies,' 'Ouest,' 'Intérieur,' 'Ouest intérieur' pour dénommer les trois provinces entre l'Ontario et la Colombie. Alsama est un acronyme à partir des mots Alberta, Saskatchewan et Manitoba. Environ la moitié de la superficie de l'Alsama se trouve dans le Nord.

Banks ou l'élevage de rennes au Mackenzie ou même les bleuetières du Pré-Nord sont des aventures à rapport très extensif.

Par ailleurs, la vastitude porte de grands inconvénients. Parmi eux, la distance qui, humainement, se mesure moins en data linéaires, qu'en coût, qu'en temps et qu'en isolement. Il en coûte environ \$2,000.00 pour transporter à Baffin une maison d'abord pré-fabriquée en Laurentie. Dans l'Arctique, le coût d'un gallon de mazout venant du Canada de base tient davantage au transport qu'à la valeur originelle du produit. Dans l'Extrême-Nord, le poids de la vastitude est accentué par l'insularisation et par un éclairement diel, limité sinon absent. Dans le premier cas, l'émiettement du relief défavorise l'établissement de voies continues de communications (pipe-line) et accentue relativement la distance à franchir; dans le second cas, la nuit polaire aggrave l'image de l'éloignement du Sud. En outre, les pénibles conditions de transport aux deux bouts de l'interglaciel, généralement situé en mai et en novembre, augmentent la distance réelle du Nord. Ces quelques exemples traduisent ce que la vastitude du Nord peut représenter pour l'homme.

Fonctions de l'écoumène

Centrer la notion de l'écoumène sur l'incidence humaine nous invite à envisager les fonctions économiques de l'espace nordique. Une typologie imaginée pour l'ensemble du Canada (Hamelin 1966) semble convenir au Nord du pays pris isolément; rappelon d'ailleurs que celui-ci occupe environ les trois-quarts de la superficie totale de celui-là. L'écoumène fonctionnel, couvrant totalement l'espace considéré, comprendrait deux grandes catégories: un écoumène actif et un écoumène passif.

(a) *L'écoumène de résidence*   L'écoumène actif, pratiquement le seul des deux à être rentable, et encore difficilement, groupe trois fonctions bien différentes. D'abord la terre nordique est utilisée pour l'habitation, ce qui constitue l'écoumène de résidence. Précisions tout de suite que l'espace habité n'échappe pas au caractère fondamental des nombreux faits nordiques, à savoir la dispersion. Pas plus ici qu'ailleurs ne faut-il voir que la distance linéaire isolant par exemple les peuplements régionaux. La dispersion s'exprime par le grand nombre des unités de peuplement. D'après Yates (1970), les 1600 maisons construites pour les Esquimaux au titre du *Northern Rental Housing Programme* l'ont été dans l'une ou l'autre des 43 agglomérations. Sans parler des camps temporaires mais usuels de chasse – cinq 'kuni' près d'noudjouac en Nouveau–Québec, sept autour de Pond Inlet, douze aux environs d'Igloolik[2] – l'on peut penser que

2   Nous estimons à un minimum de 50,000 le nombre de camps que les Indiens et

Tableau 2.1   Classement des peuplements 'arctiques,' TNO, 1971
(Statistiques du Gouvernement des Territoires-du-Nord-Ouest)

Nombre d'habitants dans l'agglomération	Nombre d'agglomérations
Moins 50 habitants	5
de 50 à 300	20
de 300 à 600	6
de 600 à 900	8
de 900 à 2800	2
Total	41

l'immense Nord canadien possède au moins 250 foyers de peuplements nordiques. S'il était permis d'établir des chiffres moyens d'habitants pour ces agglomérations, l'on arriverait à 900 âmes par poste et à une distance terrestre de 160 km entre chaque peuplement; une telle vue que montre bien le phénomène de l'émiettement de l'écoumène de résidence.

La dispersion des peuplements est en raison directe du volume démographique de ces derniers. A l'intérieur de la partie strictement 'arctique' des Territoires-du-Nord-Ouest, le tableau 2.1 fournit, par groupe de postes, la répartition de la population (16,357 habitants). Plus de la moitié des hameaux ou villages du Grand Nord n'ont pas trois cents habitants. Evidemment, les principales villes du Nord, toutes situées dans le Moyen-Nord d'ailleurs, rassemblent des populations plus considérables, mais la plus peuplée, Thompson, ne dépasse pas 25,000 habitants. Le nombre élevé des petits hameaux n'est favorable ni à l'animation régionale ni à la rentabilité des activités commerciales locales. Par contre, une telle dispersion assure une meilleure présence canadienne à l'échelle de l'ensemble des territoires.

(b) *L'écoumène d'exploitation*   Il constitue la deuxième catégorie à considérer de l'écoumène actif. Par suite de conditions structurales à voir dans la dernière section du texte, l'écoumène d'exploitation est lui aussi très étriqué dans l'espace. Partant, le gradient d'amplitude entre les môles inanimés, les espaces 'non-métropolisés' (Kayser) et les oasis d'activités primaire (extraction à Schefferville), secondaire (affineries à Flin Flon), tertiaire (services administratifs à Inuvik), ou quaternaire (bases de radar) atteint presque l'infini.

Le Nord canadien pourrait faire sien le titre d'un article de Ilmari

les Esquimaux ont fréquenté au cours de deux derniers millénaires à l'intérieur du Nord canadien. Que d'intérêt pour les racines de la canadianité! Que de recherches pour les archéologues! Que de choronymes!

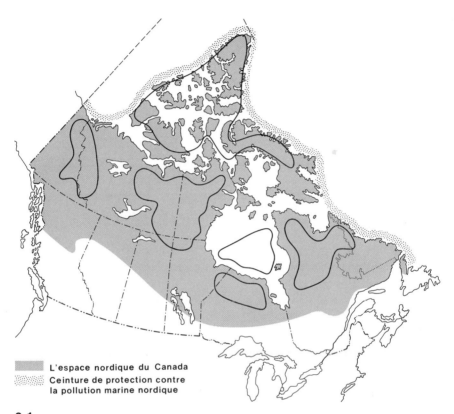

L'espace nordique du Canada
Ceinture de protection contre
la pollution marine nordique

2.1

Les Môles Principaux dans le Nord du Canada

Hustich (1968) qui décrivait la Finlande 'a developed and an undeveloped country,' Le Nord connaît tous les types d'activités économiques. Ici et là, voit-on des cas de développements équilibrés (trappage et prospection à Banks), de développement éventuel (nickle au détroit d'Hudson), de sous-développement (main d'œuvre), de mauvais développement (dégradation inutile des cultures indigènes et des terrains autour des aéroports de guerre), de surdéveloppement (menace d'épuisement de certaines réserves fauniques), enfin de régression de développement (Pré-Nord minier abitibien). Dans l'ensemble, le développement se produit davantage dans le Moyen-Nord que dans le Grand-Nord et l'Extrême-Nord. Le Nord est donc sélectif et il dégage des priorités zonales.

Un danger guette les foyers d'exploitation pionniers, c'est l'impermanence.' La mobilité caactérise le Nord autant que la disparité. Les travailleurs sont nomades en forte proportion. La demande massive de travail n'est souvent que temporaire; sa durée est limitée à la période de construction qui n'exige que peu d'années; c'est le cas de l'installation des pièces d'infrastructure: chemins de fer, quais, résidences, centrales et relais de télécommunications. Après la période de la mise en place des installations, celle de l'exploitation ne nécessitera qu'un nombre restreint d'employés, d'ailleurs facilement recrutés à même ceux qui sont déjà venus. Les autres devront repartir pour le Sud ou pour de nouveaux centres pionniers d Nord. Les chantiers créent un appel souvent irrésistible et l'‘itinérance’ des travailleurs caractérise les ‘boom towns’ du Nord du Canada. Plus grave est la mobilité des exploitations. Aux portes du Moyen-Nord, combien de chantiers forestiers, de mines et même de camps touristiques sont disparus après une trop brève existence? L'Abitibi agricole presque en entier montre un vaste abandon d'écoumène; sur 20,000 lots attribuées à des colons ou des pseudo-colons, le nombre de ‘terres’ convenablement cultivées en 1967 se fixait à 2000 seulement; pire, pour les six paroisses nées ‘agricoles’ et sises à la frontière septentrionale du peuplement abitibien, le pourcentage des fermes gagne-pain n'est plus que de 5 pour cent. Devant cette mutation, signe d'une fragilité congénitale ou de l'absence de persévérance, la présence de l'homme devient un épiphénomène. Après une ou deux générations, parfois même moins, un écoumène prostitué par des édifices taudifiés devra être l'objet d'une politique coûteuse de rénovation; autrement, ce sera le prolongement conscient d'un état de gaspillage de territoire pour lequel l'on semble avoir un penchant naturel.

(c) *L'écoumène de liaison*   Associé de près aux deux fonctions précédentes se trouve l'écoumène de liaison, dernier type de l'écoumène actif. Un regard sur la littérature indique que pour le même fait, Robinson parle de ‘transit area’ et Whebbel de ‘frontière de contact.’ On conviendra facilement qu'à partir de la dimension absolue du Nord, de la dispersion de l'habitat, de la localisation sudiste de la direction des affaires nordiques, que tout cela nécessite un réseau d'échanges relativement denses; tous les types de parcours, saisonniers ou permanents, de circulation terrestre ou de télécommunications, en viennent à former un écoumène qui touche toutes les régions du Nord, même les môles qui sont pourtant évités par l'habitation et l'exploitation. Le vol de Montréal à Frobisher traverse l'intérieur quasi vide de la péninsule du Québec-Labrador; celui de Yellowknife à Baffin sillonne le Keewatin central, tout autant désolé. Evidemment, certains couloirs sont plus achalandés; il en est ainsi de la vallée du Mackenzie, du Sud-Est du Yukon (route de l'Alaska), de la moyenne Côte-Nord du Saint-Laurent. Que l'on soit aux plans de la résidence, de l'exploitation ou des liaisons, l'écoumène du Nord n'est actif qu'à un niveau extensif.

(d) *L'écoumène passif* L'écoumène viable est moins étendu que l'écoumène passif dont les môles interrompent la continuité de l'emprise humaine. Cet écoumène apporte plutôt des pertes que des profits. Il doit être pourtant sillonné afin que les isolats, situées au-delà de lui, puissent quand même entretenir des contacts avec le Sud. Le coût élevé des transports nordiques est certes le reflet des fortes distances mais, d'une façon plus particulière il exprime la traversée des zones intermédiaires vides qui n'offrent ni passagers ni marchandises. Militairement, l'écoumène passif serait un territoire à défendre. Nous distinguons deux degrés dans l'absence de rentabilité, les môles 'peu attractifs' pouvant à l'occasion devenir des régions de secours, par exemple les basses terres hudsoniennes de l'Ontario et les môles proprement 'répulsifs' qui couvrent notamment une bonne partie des Territoires. D'est en ouest, on pourrait dénommer six régions évitées: môle québécois, môle hudsonien, môle ontarien, môle du Keewatin–Mackenzie, môle de l'archipel arctique, môle frontalier du Yukon. A l'exception de la façade septentrionale du Canada, l'on constatera que les cellules de l'écoumène passif ne touche pratiquement pas aux côtes; cette localisation réfléchit le caractère littoral et sans profondeur du peuplement au Canada. La majorité des Esquimaux habitant les rives du grand détroit péri-continental, l'*Inukland* principal est situé entre le môle de l'archipel et les môles continentaux du Yukon, du Keewatin et du Québec. Par exception, les môles peuvent comprendre certains oasis; il en est ainsi de Tungsten (150 habitants au cours de l'hiver) à la frontière du Yukon et, de Resolute sur l'île de Cornwallis au centre de l'Archipel. La vaste extension des cellules désertiques exprime les limitations de l'écoumène au plan de l'exploitation.

LES MEGAREGIONS DU NORD CANADIEN

La présence de plus de 200 petites agglomérations dispersées dans un territoire grand comme l'Europe donne certes l'impression que le Nord canadien rassemble une série de microcosmes vivant en paraposition. Il va sans dire qu'un écoumène de liaison met tous ces petits mondes isolés en contact avec le Sud, surtout en ce qui a trait à la technique et aux services sociaux. Mais dans le Nord, tout le spatial ne peut être jugé à l'échelle des petits foyers ponctuels ou linéaires de peuplement. 'La division de l'espace géographique est inséparable de la notion d'échelle,' écrivait Bertrand. L'espace total ne peut être perçu d'une seule manière et la micro-régionalisation reflète avant tout le concept de l'isolement chez les résidents.

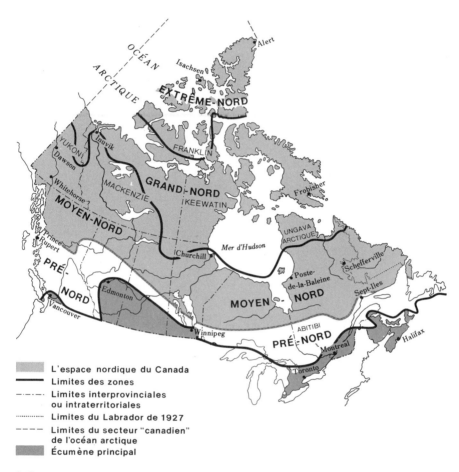

L'espace nordique du Canada
Limites des zones
Limites interprovinciales ou intraterritoriales
Limites du Labrador de 1927
Limites du secteur "canadien" de l'océan arctique
Écumène principal

2.2

Zones du Nord Canadien

Tableau 2.2   Population et densité nordique du Canada, 1966
(calcul par Hamelin et Cayouette, *Revue de Géographie de Montréal*, 1968)

Mégarégions	Nombre d'habitants	Densité en mille carré
Moyen-Nord	210,546	0.15
Grand-Nord	17,814	0.02
Extrême-Nord	140	0.007
Nord canadien	228,500	0.06

Vu à un niveau plus intégrant, l'espace nordique semble s'agencer à une série de grands ensembles, de grands univers.

Considérons l'agencement spatial suggéré par la polaricité. L'indice polaire qui nous a servi dans l'établissement des frontières du Sud (isoligne de 200 VAPO) nous permet également d'établir les pentes générales du gradient nordique et de dégager spontanément d'autres isolignes-seuils; en référence à ce dernier aspect, il en sera ainsi des traits de 500 VAPO et de 800 VAPO. L'indice nous montre que la nordicité ne s'accroit pas régulièrement vers le pôle; cette 'aggradation' monte plus rapidement du Saskatchewan au Keewatin qu'elle ne le fait de l'Alberta au Mackenzie du régions pourtant voisines du même Canada occidental. Quoiqu'il en soit, du sud vers le nord, on connaît une dégradation des conditions dites tempérées. Le Nord canadien montre trois grandes zones.

Le Moyen–Nord (Middle North)

Au-dessus du Pré-Nord que le débordement de l'écoumène principal a incorporé au Canada de base s'étend la plus vaste bande nordique individuelle du Canada, celle du Moyen-Nord; large d'environ 800 kilomètres (500 mi), cette auréole s'étire du Labrador au Yukon en englobant la baie de James. Climatiquement, c'est une région surtout subarctique. Ecologiquement, après avoir été le royaume du castor, elle est devenue le domaine des lancers pionniers, par exemple celui entre la Rivière de la Paix et le Grand lac des Esclaves. Les voies de communications, orientées 'verticalement,' caractérisent cette zone. Malheureusement, ces pénétrations linéaires ne sont cependant pas reliées sur le plan des longitudes. Cette région de plus de 200,000 habitants marque la fin de l'extension continue vers le Nord des bases sudistes. Les capitales 'territoriales' de Whitehorse et de Yellowknife sont situées dans cette bande de moyenne nordicité. Le projet du Torontois R. Rohmer, dénommé 'Mid Canada' ou 'Green North,' correspond assez bien à la région du Moyen-Nord.

Problème spatial typiquement canadien, la vaste profondeur de la zone intermédiaire entre la toundra arctique et la forêt boréale, en d'autres termes, la largeur de la zone subarctique ou de la zone du Moyen-Nord. En 1951, d'un point de vue surtout botanique, pour la péninsule du Québec–Labrador, Jacques Rousseau avait distingé du subarctique une zone hémiarctique (ou périarctique). La différenciation du Moyen-Nord est également affaire humaine et elle apparaît à l'examen de la nordicité totale; appliquée par exemple à la situation manitobaine, le large Moyen-Nord peut être subdivisé en deux: un Bas Moyen-Nord (Lower Middle North) qui sur le plan du développement tient davantage au Pré-Nord et

un Haut Moyen-Nord (Upper Middle North), bien plus près des problèmes du Grand-Nord. Ici comme en toute régionalisation géographique,
ce n'est pas un trait fin qui fait frontière, mais un limbe de transition
(carte 2.2).

Le Grand–Nord (Far North)

Le Grand-Nord a un indice de 500 à 800 vapo. C'est le Nord arctique,
plus différent du Moyen-Nord que celui-ci ne l'était du Pré-Nord. Le
Grand-Nord s'étend de part et d'autre du détroit qui sépare les îles po-
laires; il comprend à la fois des péninsules (Ungava, Keewatin), des îles
(Baffin, Victoria) et des nappes d'eau (détroit d'Hudson, golfe de Foxe,
détroit de Parry). Le Grand-Nord est plus maritime que continental. Sur
ce quart du territoire canadien, vivent moins de 20,000 habitants dont les
Esquimaux. D'après Peter Usher, à l'île de Banks, chaque trappeur exerce
son métier sur 500 milles carrés (1300 km²). L'amplitude hiver-été reste
forte. Désert d'oasis de résidence, ce pays est économiquement très dé-
ficitaire. Les dépenses des gouvernements (défense, recherche, administration, équipement) sont beaucoup plus considérables que l'engagement
du capital privé. Le Grand-Nord et l'Extrême-Nord sont un peu des
Nords d'Etat.

L'Extrême-Nord (Extreme North)

Enfin, l'Extrême-Nord couvrant moins de 10 pour cent du Canada possède une nordicité encore plus sévère: pays de glace permanente sur mer
(pack péri ou inter insulaire) ou sur terre (glaciers dont ceux d'Ellesmere) ou en profondeur (sol gelé jusqu'à plus de 500 mètres [1640 ft] à
l'île de Melville). Nansen désignait le Haut Arctique, zone de glaces
(toute l'année) et d'obscurité (hiver seulement); en fait, les nuits de 24
heures durent environ 140 jours à l'extrémité septentrionale du Canada.
C'est au travers des glaces flottantes, des chenaux de l'Extrême-Nord que
le *Manhattan* cherchait difficilement sa route au cours de l'été 1969. Une
région quasi vide à l'exception de quelques postes de présence dont Alert.

Ainsi, le Nord canadien constitue trois zones dont les frontières sont
les limbes de transition de plusieurs dizaines de kilomètres de large.

Il ne faudrait cependant pas exagérer la portée de cette zonalité. En
effet, étant donné les fréquents phénomènes de disjonction, la nordicité
est très différentielle; de grands écarts peuvent alors s'établir à l'intérieur
des zones; il peut se présenter des déviations mésorégionales de l'ordre
d'une centaine de vapo.

Une façon totalement opposée d'examiner la mégarégionalisation du
Nord partirait des projections du Canada du Sud. Comme les métropoles

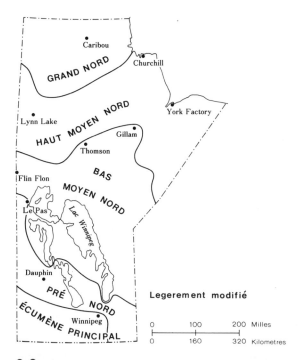

2.3

Zonation Nordique du Manitoba

sont régionales, leur flux nordique porte également régionalement. St. John's s'occupe du Labrador, Québec du Nouveau-Québec, Toronto de North Bay–Moosonee, Winnipeg de Churchill, Calgary du pétrole du Mackenzie; Edmonton est davantage que la Rivière de la Paix au départ des routes d'Alaska et de Yellowknife. Il van sans dire que les flux régionaux précédents ne sont pas les seuls à s'exercer. Certaines projections du Sud recoupent les autres. En fait, l'administration fédérale d'Ottawa irradie en toutes directions; Montréal dessert par avion et par bateau l'Est de l'Arctique. Le deuxième élément structurel de ces mégabandes longitudinales tient au caractère physique du Nord: configuration générale des terres, pénétration marine, axe fluvial, chaînes de montagnes; les traits de parcours sont venus accentuer les dispositions naturelles précédentes.

LES FORCES STRUCTURELLES

L'organisation des espaces est chose fort complexe et l'on doit se résigner à ignorer en partie le jeu invisible, subtitle ou à long terme de certains facteurs. Cette confession réaliste ne peut servir d'excuses; aussi, avons-nous identifié cinq groupes de causes qui ne jouent pas d'une manière indépendante; ces thèmes sont les dispositions naturelles, l'héritage historique, les cadres institutionnels, les forces socio-économiques et les structures mentales. Faute d'espace, nous ne traiteron que du dernier aspect qui est plus neuf.[3]

Les structures mentales

Les géographes ont l'habitude de s'intéresser peu au fait d'opinions alors que, depuis longtemps, les sociologues ont saisi l'importance des données mentales. En réalité, l'image que l'on a d'une chose devient un élément qui peut acquérir autant de poids, sinon plus, que la réalité même la plus objective. De toute façon, ce n'est qu'après avoir perçu une situation que l'on décide de ses propres comportements. A cette enseigne les Euro-canadiens ne réagissent pas de la même façon que les Amérindiens.

Le Nord chez les Euro-canadiens   Chez ces derniers, l'image mentale du Nord l'emporte sur les conditions physiques. Dans une communauté minière blanche du Moyen-Nord, une enquête récente montre que le facteur nordique perçu comme le plus important n'était ni le froid ni la neige; avant tout, c'était l'atmosphère amicale; par ailleurs, une diminution relative de l'isolement constituait le principal souhait des habitants. C'est donc, par deux termes psychologiques que ces résidents définissaient leur propre situation.

Au cours de l'histoire et au gré des interlocuteurs, l'image mentale du Nord a balotté entre deux excès: une projection idéalisée des choses ou une exagération de la pénibilité. Comme exemple du premier cas, citons à la suite et sans commentaires, la *Cathay Company* qui soutenait les entreprises de Frobisher; l'extraordinaire fièvre du Klondike qui a entraîné des participants de tous les coins du continent. Vers la première grande guerre, la publicité destinée aux colons du Nord de l'Alberta parlait de 'climat le plus sain du monde.' Une opinion fabriquée peut même aller loin et donner dans l'anti-environnement. Faudrait-il ranger au compte d'une projection idéalisée les récentes cartes du Québec qui ne reconnaissent pas du tout le Labrador terre-neuvien, pas même un Labrador côtier? Enfin, basé sur un slogan 'démocratique,' le fait pour des Blancs de ne pas admettre de distinctions socio-culturelles parmi les citoyens du Nord, c'est-à-dire de ne pas privilégier les Amérindiens; évidemment, il est plus facile d'appliquer une politique monoculturelle.

---

3   Les lecteurs désireux de voir le texte complet pourront consulter du même auteur, *Le Nord canadien comme espace*, rapport de recherches, Centre d'Etudes Nordiques de l'Université Laval à Québec, 1971, 59 pages.

A l'opposé, le Nord plutôt d'ètre idéalisé au-delà de ce qu'il est a subi des critiques parfois bien exagérées. Sans rappeler les célèbres propos pisse-vinaigre de Voltaire, le Nord a été victime de mythes d'indifférence, sinon de répulsion. Les explorateurs et les missionnaires qui ont œuvré au cours de périodes que l'on pourrait qualifiées de prétechniques ont laissé l'idée d'un pays sévère. La pénibilité crainte est venue accentuer la pénibilité réelle. L'on rejoint facilement la boutade de Stefansson à savoir que dans le Nord 'les problèmes imaginaires sont plus importants que les problèmes réels.' L'image du Nord semble déprécier encore la réalité et une enquête récente auprès de 43 étudiants de géographie de l'Ontario méridional mentionnait la façade arctique comme la principale région canadienne où aucun d'entre eux ne voudrait vivre (C.A.G. Waterloo 1971).

Cependant, l'appréciation des choses évolue. Les attitudes prises et à prendre concernant l'écoumène d'exploitation manifeste non simplement une évolution mentale mais une évolution dans une noble direction. Ici l'on pourrait isoler trois conceptions ou trois étapes. Pour les Esquimaux d'avant les Blancs, la terre ou les chenaux ne fournissaient que le 'support' à l'exploitation faunique. Au cours d'une première phase de la modernité, le territoire est devenue 'matière première,' c'est-à-dire minerais, bois dont l'exploitation pouvait assurer des profits. Depuis peu, la terre est considérée comme un 'patrimoine'; elle n'est plus une 'commodity' d'extraction jusqu'à destruction; elle devient un élément à respecter pour les générations futures suivant le slogan: que la pollution ne tue pas la qualité de l'environnement! Cette nouvelle attitude, sans doute influencée par les scientistes, met en honneur la conscience de l'homme.

Le Nord chez les Amérindien   Jusqu'à très récemment, la terre des Esquimaux était un fait familial et local mais très peu national et continental. Les Indiens, plus nombreux et parfois plus structurés politiquement, semblaient entretenir une conscience plus nette de l'ensemble des terres de leurs tribus. Les quelques Traités passés avec les Blancs réfléchissent probablement une façon d'apprécier l'écoumène. Depuis peu et chez tous les groupes des Indigènes, la 'territorialité' s'est grandement développée; alors qu'auparavant les Blancs pouvaient tout au plus reconnaître chez les Amérindiens de timides définitions ethnosociales de leurs territoires, maintenant, les Indigènes eux-mêmes veulent se donner une définition territoriale de leur société.

Cette évolution pourrait créer une situation très difficile. En effet, généralement les Euro-canadiens continuent à agir comme s'ils étaient les seuls propriétaires des terres. Or, les prétentions amérindiennes remettent en cause une question apparemment résolue. Devant cette nouvelle réclamation, il sera difficile aux Blancs de ne pas reconnaître aux Indigènes des droits plus étendus sur les terres dont leurs ancêtres ont vécu. Par ailleurs, il est plus que douteux que les Amérindiens réussissent à redevenir les uniques dominateurs du Nord canadien. Il va sans dire que face au code, il faille distinguer entre les régions; Territoire indien de 1774, Réserves, domaines qui ont fait l'objet de traités; sections qui n'en ont pas fait l'objet, par exemple l'*Inukland*. La question la plus compliquée est d'évaluer de combien les ancêtres étaient 'propriétaires' de leur écoumène de parcours et de chasse.

Chez les Amérindiens, au-delà du problème fondamental de l'identité territoriale se pose celui de la culturalité de cet écoumène. Le fait d'introduire des aspects culturels dans la définition de l'espace indigène n'est pas un concept qui aurait pu être emprunté à l'anglophonie nord-américaine: celle-ci dont la langue est bien établie met plutôt l'accent sur les événements économiques et administratifs de l'espace. A propos de l''Amérindie,' la principale difficulté ne vient pas de la multiplicité des langues; destinées au Québec et utilisant seulement les principaux véhicules, les recommandations du rapport français de la Commission Dorion sur les Indiens ont été quatre fois traduites: en montagnais, en cri, en iroquois et en esquimau. La difficulté vient plutôt du danger que représente l'acculturation prolongée. Les Euro-canadiens, si ce n'est par exception (les missionnaires), ont encore moins respecté les cultures indigènes que les territoires de chasse. Pour un, les Indigènes ont été scolarisés suivant la langue des gouvernements; même dans le Nouveau-Québec, c'est en anglais que la majorité des Esquimaux sont instruits dans les écoles. Dans les régions où dominent les Indigènes, le facies linguistique officiel de l'écoumène ne réfléchit donc pas la langue du cœur.

Mais la langue de l'école, de la radio et de l'évolution possède le prestige énorme de la modernité. Les Indigènes, suivant l'expression d'un poète esquimau, sont comme des moustiques qu'attire un globe lumineux; ils ne refuseront pas les traits de la culture dominante de l'Amérique du Nord. L'on peut également penser que la plupart des Amérindiens n'accepteront pas d'abandonner la majorité de leurs traits culturels. Ainsi les Indigènes devront réaliser une synthèse entre des valeurs traditionnelles d'hérédité ou d'identité et des valeurs nouvelles de mutation et d'acquisition. S'ils ne sont adéquatement préparés pour aborder ainsi l'évolution de leur écoumène culturel, ils peuvent, et dans leurs propres termes, demander à l'Euro-canadien compréhension et collaboration.

3 Transportation in the Canadian North

MICHAEL MARSDEN

It is generally accepted that the development and settlement of the Canadian North has been severely restricted by the absence of an adequate transportation net. Although there are severe physical handicaps in terms of a harsh climate and rugged terrains, with muskeg, permafrost, and a variety of other well-understood impediments to the construction and operation of transportation systems, these conditions are not the true constraints. Steam vessels plied the Yukon River in the 1860s and development of the Mackenzie waterways begun in 1920 was based upon fur trade routes more than a century old. A railway was built across the Coast Range and into Yukon Territory in 1900 and still operates routinely through winter temperatures of −50°C (−58°F) and over sections with 1300 cm (43 ft) of snow per annum; while aircraft were successfully operated in the Mackenzie District during 1921, and were used routinely throughout the north after 1925.

Some physical problems are serious, such as the severely restricted season for shipping, but in general the real problems are economic, and usually they are common to any frontier area. Many are prosaic. One example is the matter of sheer distance in the Canadian North. If a complete transportation net did exist, and if it could be operated at costs equivalent to those outside, any producer would still have difficulty competing with suppliers closer to the markets of the south. Another well-known factor which is, nevertheless, frequently underestimated is the small scattered population to be served. With 50,000 people distributed across 4½ million square kilometres (1½ million sq mi), the Northwest Territories has a population density of 0.02 persons per square mile and the Yukon Territory 0.07. Of some 70 settlements existing in 1968, one-half had less than 350 inhabitants and only six had more than 1000, while the largest, Whitehorse, Y.T., had 10,800.

Furthermore, while support systems took into the North considerable amounts, there was no back haul. All of Canada's truly arctic ports were built to receive only. Planes returned empty as did trucks, trains, and barges, thus doubling the cost for the consumer. This trend began to reverse in 1955 on the White Pass and Yukon Railway and on the Great Slave Lake Railway in 1969, but ironically the expected developments which will see large exports of oil and minerals will merely reverse the imbalance, resulting in essentially one-way traffic outbound, and it is not possible to foresee balanced hauls and optimal tariffs in any sector.

Marine Transportation

The northern seas, including the coastal and interior waters, are frozen and impassable by conventional vessels during as much as eleven months of the year as has been noted in the first chapter. Other environmental hazards are wind storms which may occur during spring and fall, accentuating difficulties in ice operations, and in some areas fog, triggered by warm open water. For example, Nottingham and Resolution islands at the west and east ends of Hudson Strait may have as many as 18 days of fog a month between June and September.

The net result is that ocean transport is restricted to late July, August, September, and early October, with different periods in each sector, and with slight variations in the season from year to year. The marine routes available are effectively limited to those actually in use (Figure 3.1).

Conventional operations during the established season have become reliable, and there is an adequate knowledge of bathymetry, currents, ice conditions, and meteorology along all routes. Navigational aids, including radar beacons, have been installed and are maintained by the Marine Works Branch of DOT, but they are probably not adequate to serve any sustained increase in commercial traffic. The federal Department of Transport is the co-ordinator for all freight moving into the eastern Arctic and the Archipelago, and through its Marine Operations Branch and the Canadian Coast Guard it organizes and undertakes annual sealifts. During the sealift, Coast Guard icebreakers (all equipped for survey and research and with some cargo capacity) accompany chartered commercial and rate-per-ton vessels, usually from Montreal, in a series of voyages that deliver heavy supplies to all the accessible sites in the eastern Arctic. Cargo rates vary according to the delivery site, but in general they relate to latitude. South of 70° rates averaged slightly less than 4 cents a ton/mile in 1969; north of 70° they averaged 5 cents a ton/mile. The schedule of operations and the obtaining rates are made available yearly, in advance, from the Marine Services Division, DOT, Ottawa.

Western Arctic ocean shipping is closely integrated with the Mackenzie River transportation system. Traffic in the area has increased and since 1960 DOT has assigned the icebreaker *Camsell* to the route.

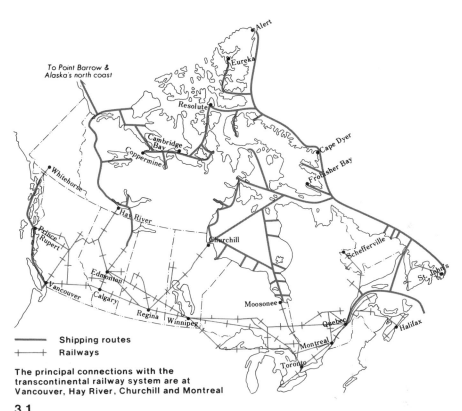

3.1

Canada's Northern Shipping Routes

Marine transport in this sector has become the responsibility of the sole common carrier on the Mackenzie River, Northern Transportation Company Ltd., a crown corporation. Most freight comes down the river and is then handled by two coastal vessels, or by three ocean-going 4000 h.p. tugs and steel barges which offer advantages in the shoal conditions common to this area. They are designed to carry bulk cargo, or deck loads with capacities between 70 and 700 tons. Since costs on the river system drop with distance and there is no differential rate charge, on reaching the sea all materials shipped from the railway at Hay River, N.W.T., or Fort McMurray, Alberta, are moving at the lowest rates when they reach the ocean sector, about 7 cents a ton/mile.

Eastern Arctic marine traffic during 1969 involved 12 Coast Guard vessels (7 icebreakers), 4 dry cargo vessels, 7 oil tankers and 10 chartered ships, delivering slightly more than 100,000 tons of freight and fuel.

Because the potential demands upon shipping far surpass the present reality, it is worth reviewing some recent experiments and estimates aimed at the immediate future. A study made for the Department of Indian Affairs and Northern Development in 1970 (Warnock Hersey 1970) identified potential production totalling 10 million tons of mineral ores and 120 million barrels of oil each year for periods of up to 30 years.

During 1969, the U.S. tanker *Manhattan* traversed the North West Passage late in the season to Prudhoe Bay, Alaska, from the U.S. eastern coast. A second voyage in mid-winter (early 1971) was not so successful. The *Manhattan*, 940 ft long (287 m), 110,000 tons deadweight tonnage, and 43,000 h.p., had a specially constructed ice-breaking bow and some reinforcement in the hull and machinery. The sheer size of the vessel gives it an ability to move at will through ice up to 15 ft (5 m) thick and proposals in 1970/1 were for vessels up to 250,000 D.W.T. with engines of 100,000 h.p., or three times that normally used in such vessels. Detailed figures are available for the cost of building and operating oil and dry bulk carriers as well as modification costs for existing vessels.

An estimate presented to a symposium on Arctic and Middle North Transportation (Cass *in* Sater 1969) for shipping between Prudhoe Bay and the U.S. Atlantic ports, postulated twelve 250,000 D.W.T. tankers, each with a helicopter for ice reconnaissance operating on a five-week turnaround schedule. They would cost $45,000,000 each and the fleet would move 15,000,000 tons of oil per year at a cost one half of that in the southern pipeline systems (the Arctic Transportation Study estimates 0.041 cents per ton/mile exclusive of insurance profit and contingencies) or one tenth of the cost in an arctic pipeline. Nevertheless, in 1971 pipelines have been gaining preference over the marine concept for a variety of short-term reasons including high insurance. A major cost item for all arctic shipping is the extremely high insurance costs shown in Figure 3.2. Note that the premiums increase outside the 'normal season' and for voyages terminating north or west of Resolute.

A familiar variant to avoid commitment of capital to short-term projects is the intensive use of large chartered vessels over the brief open period to move extremely large tonnages. A further variant was the plan to ship iron ore from the Mary River site on Baffin Island with a large fleet which would move a year's production in two months, on a short haul to a nearby year-round port like Godhaab, Greenland, whence it could be shipped conventionally throughout the year, either by the same vessels on longer runs, or by routine shipping. In practice the idea needs precise costing since it involves stockpiling twice with the attendant handling costs and the cost of inventory (Figure 3.3). Furthermore it assumes that the charter operators have alternative traffic for the remainder of the year which may not be the case on the scales envisaged.

River Transportation

River transportation has been effectively confined to the Mackenzie waterways since the Yukon River service was discontinued in 1955. The Mackenzie River with a drainage basin of 700,000 square miles (1813 km²) drains a large part of the three western provinces and both Territories. It carried 2400 miles (3860 km) of scheduled shipping routes in 1970, and gave access to another 1500 miles (2410 km) of coastal shipping (Figure 3.4). Until the 1930s all heavy freight was carried by stern-wheel steamboats, as on the Yukon, and the capacity was small, but the growth of mining throughout the 30s on Great Bear Lake, Great Slave Lake, and Lake Athabasca encouraged a constant growth in river traffic, which was handled by tug and barge operations.

There are only two barriers to shipping on the entire drainage system, portages being necessary around a 25-mile (40 km) sector of the Slave River near Fort Smith, and another of 9 miles (15 km) around rapids on the Great Bear River. Because of these obstacles, the service is generally described in three sectors, known as the Athabasca area, the Mackenzie ara, and the Great Bear Lake area.

Climatic conditions are severe and winter freezing limits the season. In the Athabasca area movement does not usually begin before the middle of May, while Great Slave Lake cannot be used before the middle of June, and Great Bear Lake before mid-July. When the open season ends, shipping is closed out in the reverse order, movements on Great Bear Lake and the lower Mackenzie ending late in September and on Great Slave Lake by mid-October, with a final closing of all navigation on the Slave and Athabasca rivers at the end of October. Normally the 1100 miles (1780 km) between Hay River and Tuktoyaktuk take 9 days northbound, 12 days southbound.

Because of the size of the collecting basin, there are major variations in water levels in the different sectors at different times in the year. Heavy spring runoff from snow melt gives high water levels everywhere, but subsequently the subhumid environment causes declining levels in late summer. In the Athabasca area tugs and barges are designed to a limiting draught of 2½ feet (76.2 cm), but the barges may be loaded to a 6-foot (183-cm) draught and carry a great deal more during high-water periods. The Mackenzie water levels are consistently deeper and vessels there have a maximum draught of 6½ feet (198 cm) set, not by normal channel depths, but by five rapids which all occur near the Hay River terminal

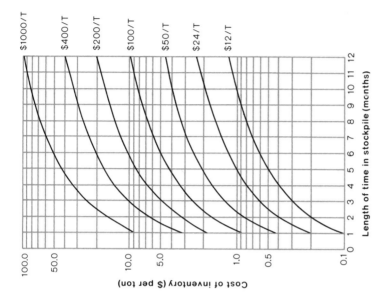

Length of time in stockpile (months)

Cost of inventory ($ per ton)

$1000/T

$400/T

$200/T

$100/T

$50/T

$24/T

$12/T

3.3

Calculated Cost of Stockpile Inventory for Ores with Production Costs between $12 and $1000 per Ton

(Source: Arctic Transportation Study 1970)

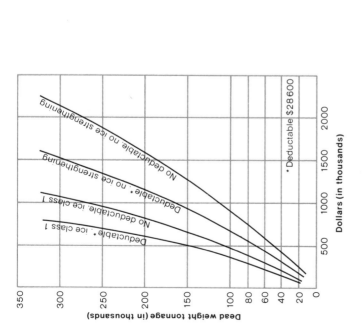

Dead weight tonnage (in thousands)

Dollars (in thousands)

Deductable* ice class 1

No deductable* ice class 1

Deductable* no ice strengthening

No deductable no ice strengthening

*Deductable $28 600

This graph shows additional premium for voyage during normal shipping period - 23 July to 10 October

3.2

Additional Premiums for an Arctic Voyage to Resolute Area

(Source: Arctic Transportation Study 1970)

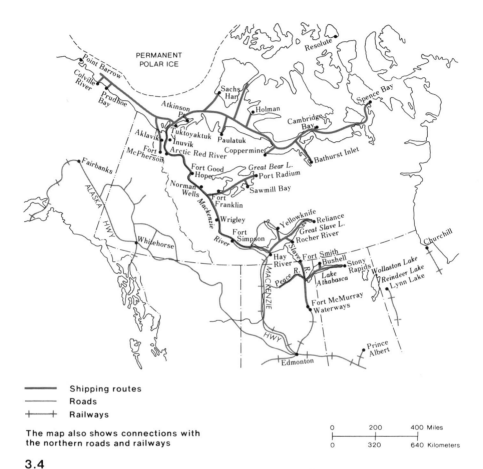

Shipping routes
Roads
Railways

The map also shows connections with
the northern roads and railways

| 0 | 200 | 400 Miles |
| 0 | 320 | 640 Kilometers |

3.4

Shipping Routes of the Northern Transportation Company 1971

and thus limit capacity over the entire system. The restrictions are emphasized in times of drought, and the Bennett Dam on the Peace River
seems to have reduced flow slightly, so that in 1970 the sector operated
at only 60 per cent of design capacity. Senior officers of NTC have proposed that these obstructions be dredged to a depth of 8 ft (244 cm) and
a clear width of 350 ft (107 m), increasing to 700 ft (213 m) on turns,
to allow the passage of a more economical barge train, a six barge tow in
a 3 × 2 pushing configuration. Such a tow would be 170 ft (52 m) wide,
670 ft (204 m) long and would carry 10,000 tons of freight. Some dredging has been done, but the full program would take 3 years and cost 16
million dollars.

Great Bear Lake has 500 miles (805 m) of routeway with unlimited depth, but the river that drains the lake deteriorates into a series of swift currents and boulder-strewn rapids, limiting draught to a mere 26 inches (66 cm) before reaching an impassable rapid that requires a 9-mile (15 km) portage. The difficulty of bringing even empty vessels up this section has set an upper limit of 6 feet (183 cm) loaded for the barges on the lake.

Early tugboats had very little power (60 h.p. in some cases), and they towed wooden barges of great weight. The modern trend is for tugs with up to 4000 h.p. and relatively light steel barges. Barge capacity has increased from 100 to 1000 tons, and tows have risen from 400 or 500 tons in one string to 6000 tons and more, the ability to handle large strings being important in view of the limiting depths. Since 1950 there has been a program of aids to navigation in the form of newly surveyed charts, a river 'Pilot,' navigational aids in all channels, and dredging at selected sites. The program was accelerated in the 1960s.

The only common carrier in the area today is the Northern Transportation Company Ltd. In 1970 they operated 28 tugs, three of them ocean-going, 145 steel barges with capacities up to 1500 tons, including refrigerated units for perishable goods, and two coastal vessels. They maintain receiving depots at Fort McMurray, Alberta, and Hay River, N.W.T., with suitable facilities for storing and handling heavy equipment. There is a trans-shipment facility at Tuktoyaktuk which includes a floating dry dock, and major freight handling facilities at Yellowknife, Bear River, Norman Wells, and Inuvik. In addition, they maintain ship construction and repair facilities at Hay River, Fort McMurray, and Fort Smith.

Northern Transportation began as a small private company in 1931 with a wooden tug and two barges, operating between Hay River and Aklavik. It extended service to the Eldorado mine at Port Radium in 1933, and after changing to its present name in 1934 was acquired by Eldorado Gold Mines Ltd., thus becoming a crown corporation when the parent company was nationalized in 1944. In 1947 it absorbed the traffic left when a HBC subsidiary, Hudson's Bay Transport, gave up its function as a common carrier and restricted itself to its own resupply. In 1963 it took over even that role at the request of HBC. In 1965 Yellowknife Transportation Co. Ltd., Arctic Shipping Ltd., and Decury Supply Ltd. were acquired in what was essentially a rationalization of somewhat inefficient competition by parallel services in the period after the Mackenzie Highway reached Yellowknife.

NTC handled some 28,000 tons of freight in 1946. In 1969 it handled

250,000 tons, expected 300,000 in 1971, and forecast 750,000 tons in 1975 (NTC *Annual Report* 1970). General commodity freight rates in 1969 decreased sharply with distance up to 500 miles (805 km). At this point they levelled off, costing about 20 cents a ton/mile over the first hundred miles, dropping to 7 cents a ton/mile over the first thousand. Although the company has made a profit in every year since 1944, and has been reducing tariffs for 20 years, operations showed a loss in 1969 which was attributed to debt servicing for new capital equipment.

There are two important characteristics of the river system. First, the main function is to link the western Arctic and sub-Arctic to the national road and rail networks of the south. A crude road was cleared in the winter of 1938/9 linking the Mackenzie District via Hay River to the Northern Alberta Railway at Grimshaw, and was used to haul supplies for Yellowknife during the first gold strike. Freight was hauled on sleds by heavy tractors at first, and then at the end of World War II the 'cat-road' was improved to highway standards at a cost of 4½ million dollars. Trucking companies began to haul materials to Hay River for shipment by barge to Yellowknife or down the Mackenzie.

Today there is no need to transfer at either Grimshaw or Hay River since the Great Slave Lake Railway goes through to Hay River and the Mackenzie Highway reaches to Yellowknife. But there has been no complete swing to rail use yet, partly because shippers have to take box-car loads, and partly because many items enter the general area by truck, not train. Trucks of Byers Transport and Grimshaw Trucking still supply significant tonnages along this route, even to the Pine Point mine itself. The highway has not eliminated barge traffic to Yellowknife, and although it is ten years since the road reached Yellowknife all bulk supplies are still taken in by barge. It remains to been seen how traffic will finally be allocated, but it seems that in a time of expanding traffic each type will carry more, possibly with distinctively specialized functions.

The second characteristic thus emerging is that the river traffic cannot be viewed in isolation and that there is a marked trend towards integrated systems. Originally the different carriers trans-shipped bulk materials from one mode to another, with high labour costs at every break point. Trucking companies moved first, to the piggyback semi-trailers which could come into Grimshaw on a rail flatcar, be hauled by road to Hay River, and then on barges of the Yellowknife Transportation Co. to Yellowknife. More recently some containers are being used and some river barges have been adapted to take them as deck cargo.

More than one-half of all the river freight has consisted of bulk oil, but since it consists of refined products there is no fear of the effect of a Mackenzie pipeline. Indeed, the construction of such a line would use the barge system for the transport of construction supplies and NTC using its experience in Alaska, has prepared sites for handling and storage. The river is potentially the best route too for supplies for an Alaskan pipeline, with a distance from railhead less than one-half that of any alternative.

Air Transportation

The environment offers few problems for the scheduled lines since Canadian operators are habituated to winter cold and snow, but it does offer a variety of problems for those aircraft which do not use conventional landing fields but are operated as 'bush planes,' usually under charter, to go anywhere required.[1]

The best period for flying in the Arctic is late winter, when there are increasing amounts of daylight, ice surfaces are intact and hard, and the weather, although cold, is clear and moderating daily. Later, sectors of open water increase the likelihood of fog and low cloud formations and, since the freezing level is always near the ground, icing conditions are common. High summer brings open water in late June, July, and August. Consequently, float planes may utilize lakes, rivers, and the sea, and visibility is generally good for all flying. Skis become useless as the snow softens and melts off, usually in June, and wheeled aircraft may have trouble with the soft active layer above the permafrost during summer. The late summer conditions improve as the land dries out, and freeze-up in September shows further improvement for wheeled landings. However, by that time conditions are deteriorating and the amount of daylight is decreasing rapidly, an undesirable factor in the mounting of large operations where delays could become critical.

During winter and spring, snow-covered lake or river ice is preferred for landings since snow-covered tundra or boulder fields offer treacherous surfaces for landing or taxiing. One metre of fresh water ice is needed to support the shock of the lightest aircraft, but two will support most aircraft flying today. Sea ice is a problem because there is a variety of types and the salts incorporated lower the unit strength. Some sea ice will support all landings at two metres (6.7 ft), while other ice, formed under different conditions is totally inadequate. Sea ice is most unpredictable during warmer periods since it loses strength rapidly above $-8°C$ ($+18°F$).

1 There is a good brief account from an operations point of view in *The Arctic Basin* (Sater 1969).

Generally speaking float operations are confined to the Shield areas and the rivers and lakes of the west where there is abundant open water in the season. Planes on floats pay a severe penalty in terms of weight and aerodynamic efficiency. Skis also offer a weight and drag penalty, although larger aircraft, like the DC3 and L130 may have retractable skis. Ski-wheels which offer the pilot a choice are the most common winter configuration, allowing landings on prepared or unprepared sites at will, but they are heavy, relatively expensive, and may demand strengthened undercarriages. During break-up and freeze-up all aircraft may be restricted to prepared runways.

In winter and early spring sea-smoke may rise as high as 1500 metres (4921 ft) although it normally hugs the water, while in extreme cold the water may sublimate, giving a poor visibility condition called ice-haze. A much more serious hazard is blowing snow (blizzard) since, although the snow rarely reaches more than 15 metres (49 ft) from the surface, it may totally obscure visibility for a pilot on the strip at exactly the crucial altitudes in landing or take-off, and airfields are occasionally closed because of it.

Extreme cold requires modifications to even the simplest servicing routine, and $-40°C$ ($-40°F$) is regarded as a critical temperature. If aircraft are stored outside, they require heating of the engine and cabin controls before take-off, which may require three or more hours. Some strips provide nose-shelters for the purpose, but portable heaters, hoses, and hoods are needed for field use.

Charter aircraft carry more freight than the scheduled lines in the Canadian North, exceeding 20,000 tons in most years. The prime characteristic of the charter craft is versatility and most such aircraft have STOL (short take-off and landing) characteristics and can operate from airfields with minimal facilities, to land upon open ground, snow, or ice – with floats on lakes, rivers, and the sea. The most unusual are Pipers, Cessnas, and Beavers which have large, light, low-pressure tires which can land almost anywhere and have supplanted helicopters for all but VTOL (vertical take-off and landing) operations because they are much cheaper.

The most successful planes are deHavilland's Beaver and Otter and their variants, with payloads between 1500 and 4000 lbs (680–1814 kg). They are durable, reliable utility transports with simple maintenance, good STOL characteristics and modest operating costs. The ton/mile cost to a user for the Beaver, Otter, and Twin Otter would be about 130 cents, 100 cents, and 70 cents, respectively, the direct operating cost (DOC) being much less.

All charter rates are controlled by zone and published by DOT. A Cessna 180 charters for 55–65 cents a mile, Beavers at 80–100 cents, Turbo-Beavers at 95–115 cents, Otters at 120–155 cents, and Twin Otters at 130–160 cents; the higher rates in all cases being for the most remote zones.

The extreme range of aircraft now operating is from the Piper Super Cub with a payload of 200 lbs (91 kg) and a range of 240 miles (386 km) to the roomy, easily loaded Lockheed LC 130F Hercules, with a 30,000 lb (13,610 kg) payload and a 5600 miles (9010 km) round-trip capability. Of the larger aircraft only the Bristol Freighter and the Hercules have ski-wheel ability.

For larger quantities of freight and more economical rates the larger aircraft are necessary. They normally operate to prepared strips on earth, ice, or snow, the preparation being little more than a rough levelling by bulldozer of strips 3000 to 6000 feet (914–1829 m) long. DC3s, Bristol Freighters, and Hercules have, however, been operated routinely to totally unprepared sites.

Robins (1969) has outlined the growth of heavy air freighting. The construction of the Distant Early Warning radar defence net marked the turning point and aircraft moved 61 million pounds of freight. Those operations were backed by a sealift so that fuel was available for return flights, but later civilian projects, e.g. the import of materials for a school at Cambridge Bay, had to carry fuel for the return, a serious depletion of payload and a source of increased cost to be added to the one-way haul. Nevertheless, in 1960 when 60 tons of supplies were airlifted to Coppermine after a sealift failed, the operation was so successful that a number of communities turned to aircraft resupply, and the 1968 airlift took in 2000 tons of supplies and materials. At different times aircraft were used to open and operate the Taurcanis Mine in the barrens, supply an oil-drilling program on Bathurst Island, and export 200,000 lbs (90,700 kg) of char from Cambridge Bay.

It has become clear that modern aircraft operating under optimal conditions would undercut or equal most other modes of transportation. A Boeing 747f with full freight on both legs or a round trip would, according to the manufacturer's figures, be less expensive than all other means but river barge and pipeline. A more realistic figure, one that allows for indirect costs and a 60 per cent load factor, still leaves the modern aircraft in close competition on a cost per ton/mile basis with railways and trucks (Table 3.1).

Helicopters have proved expensive to operate and their limited speed, range, and payload are restrictive. Consequently, they are now used only

Table 3.1   Comparative ton/mile rates for different transportation modes
(from: Weick and Merrill 1969, p. 70)

Mode	Vehicle or craft	Cost/ton mile (in cents)
Air cushion vehicles	SRN 6	100
	Hovermarine HM$_2$ (sidewall type)	50
Tractor train		100
Aircraft	G$_4$ Helicopter (load 500 lbs)	400
	Helicopter (load 3–4 tons)	125
	Helicopter (load 10 tons)	50
	deHavilland Otter	100
	DH Twin Otter	70
	DH Beaver	130
	Bristol	30
	C130 Hercules	15
	Boeing 747f	5
	Boeing tilt wing (20 ton load)	30
Truck	Standard highway vehicle on winter road	20
	Standard highway vehicle on highway	8
Rail	Standard equipment (northern railways)	7
Marine	Ships on northern supply operations	5
	Barge in Mackenzie	4
	Super tanker in Arctic	?
	Cargo submarine in Arctic	?
Pipeline	Standard in south	1
	Northern pipeline	?

NOTE: The ton/mile rates for aircraft and ACV's would double if the craft returned with no load.

for operations which utilize their VTOL characteristics to the full, e.g. in support of marine operations where they can land on deck and are invaluable for ice reconnaissance and ship-to-shore, ship-to-ship transfers when bad ice conditions prevail. Because of their limited range, helicopters need back-up support for long-range operations and have even been flown north inside large aircraft and out again at the end of the season. They are generally operated on soft buoyant pontoons which allow them to land on water, snow, ice, rock, boulders, or wood and steel platforms, but impose a penalty in payload and drag. In 1970 a sealift experimented with a Sikorsky 'flying crane' to replace conventional lightering to the beach. It could overfly ice-infested shoals, cross the beach, and offload at the warehouse, saving handling costs and time. No cost figures are available, but the concept may be promising since the craft is designed to take pre-loaded containers and winch them up into space in an otherwise skeletal airframe.

All costing depends upon the assumptions, but Weick and Merrill (1969) suggest $4.00 a ton/mile for a small helicopter like the Bell G13 with a 500 lb (227 kg) payload, $1.25 a ton/mile for craft in the 3 and 4 ton payload range (Boeing-Vertol 107), and 50 cents a ton/mile for the biggest craft. There are no figures for such revolutionary vehicles as the Russian Mi-12 helicopter now flying, with a claimed payload of 90,000 lbs (40,820 kg), but such vehicles might change the cost pattern drastically.

The common charter points have been Frobisher Bay, Churchill, Yellowknife, and Whitehorse, but a significant number of carriers such as Atlas Aviation may operate seasonally from a northern field like Resolute and once operational may be chartered from that point (Figure 3.5). Small aircraft are available also at Cambridge Bay, Fort Simpson, Fort Smith, Hay River, Inuvik, Norman Wells, and Sawmill Bay. Aircraft with capacities over 18,000 lbs (8160 kg) must be chartered in the south and rates will include the flight in and out. *Prospectus: North of 60°* suggests that all fares and freight rates run between 20 and 50 per cent higher in the north.

Because of the construction of new airfields and the improvement of old landing strips, and because of an incentive program which pays 50 per cent of the cost of an 'exploratory aerodrome' up to $20,000 and 50 per cent of 'pre-production aerodromes' up to $100,000, there is a rapid increase in the sophistication of aircraft which can enter the North. Nordair, for example, is operating Boeing 737s into Resolute, and the North could now use the new generation jet freighters like the Douglas DC8-63F and the Boeing 747f which can be operated with only 60 per cent utilization for less than 10 cents ton/mile. When demand is big enough and reliable enough, air freighting will be hard to displace, especially when it offers speed and continuity in comparison to slow, seasonal, marine freight even at 5 cents a ton/mile.

Railway Transportation

Apart from the railways that exploit the iron ores of Nouveau-Québec and Labrador and lie wholly within Quebec, there are only three lines that enter or serve the far North. Each railway has a different character, both in the terrains traversed and in the functions intended or carried out.

The Hudson Bay Railway between The Pas, Manitoba, and Churchill was built to provide an outlet for western farm produce, specifically wheat

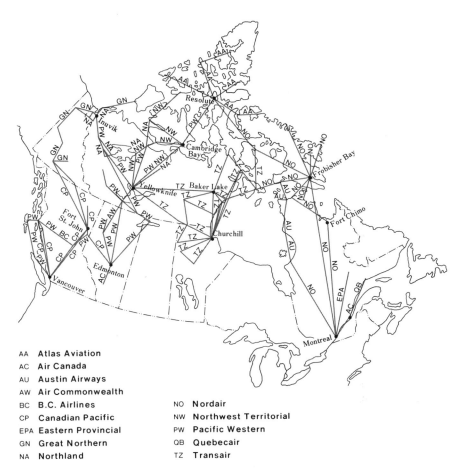

AA   Atlas Aviation
AC   Air Canada
AU   Austin Airways
AW   Air Commonwealth
BC   B.C. Airlines
CP   Canadian Pacific
EPA Eastern Provincial
GN   Great Northern
NA   Northland

NO   Nordair
NW   Northwest Territorial
PW   Pacific Western
QB   Quebecair
TZ   Transair

3.5

Northern Air Carriers and their Scheduled Routes 1971

which was sensitive to freight rates. By using Hudson Strait shipping to Europe there would be a saving, compared with the Great Lakes–Montreal route, of 474 miles (763 km) from Winnipeg and 1142 miles (1838 km) from Edmonton. The line later proved vital in the development of the eastern Arctic, bringing bulk supplies for trans-shipment by sea and air. The history of its construction and early operation is given in detail by Fleming (1957).

Modern operation, the responsibility of Canadian National Railways, is much more effective than in the past. The line was dieselized in 1950 and there are two passenger trains in each direction each week, with freight carriers when required. Spurs serve the huge mines at Thompson and Lynne Lake, and in 1969, 586,000 tons of wheat were moved to 28 ships. Churchill is beginning to change its one-way characteristics by importing oil and machinery. The oil is for northern use, but there is now some freight going inland.

The function of the port at Churchill is undoubtedly a restriction upon the efficiency of the railway. For example, unit trains, the most economical means of handling regular shipments of a uniform commodity were evaluated in 1970 and 1971 and it became clear that they would not be effective given the seasonal character of the port and the relatively small tonnages shipped in the short open season.

The shipping volume has not reached early expectations because of the short port season, high marine insurance, and because most vessels have a one-way haul which increases the effective tariffs. High insurance premiums eliminated the cost advantage of the first commercial voyages in 1931 although their success started a series of reductions. Premiums were halved for 1932 but only for the season 10 August–30 September and any extension was expensive. Even today, with considerable experience on the route and with the harbour open technically between early June and mid-November, the normal season for insurance is 26 July to 10 October. This restriction on the usable period is reflected in small total tonnages per year. At one time frustrated growers seriously suggested incorporating to operate an uninsured fleet of vessels.

Furthermore, Churchill is essentially a single commodity port and since there is only brief seasonal employment, stevedores and elevator operators must be brought in from outside and handling costs are high, sometimes five times that in Montreal harbour. Because of the port characteristics, and in spite of subsidies on rates, the railway shows a net operating loss every year.

The Great Slave Lake Railway completed in 1966 was ostensibly built to exploit the large lead–zinc deposits at Pine Point, known since 1896, but the route chosen links the Mackenzie barge system to the transcontinental railway system and also serves a pioneer agricultural community. Although the Pine Point properties are owned by a subsidiary of the Canadian Pacific Railway, it was apparently unwilling to build a line, probably in the belief that no revenues would accrue. However, governmental policies since 1957 had emphasized access, and as a result of a Royal Commission the decision was made in 1961 to pay Canadian National $86,250,000 to build and operate a line, with another $12,500,000 to come from Pine Point Mines Ltd. with the company committed to shipping 215,000 tons of ore concentrates per year for ten years.

The 377 mile (542 km)-route from Roma on the Northern Alberta Railway to Hay River on Great Slave Lake was completed ahead of schedule and for less than the estimated cost in 1966, with a spur of 55 miles (86 km) to the Pine Point mine. The locomotives and stock are conventional with routine modifications for northern work, except that the ore cars are built to conform to the physical requirements of the smelter at Trail, B.C.

Critical points in the decision had been the selection of a route that traversed 13,000,000 acres (5,260,000 ha) of usable forest and 6,000,000 acres (2,430,000 ha) of farm land, only 700,000 acres (283,000 ha) of which were being used in the Peace River sector; and the ability of the line to allow heavy freight to bypass the barge portage at Fort Smith. That the concepts were correct was shown by 1970 when CNR could claim that traffic generated by developments other than the mine had equalled the ore tonnage (Bandeen 1969), and the Great Slave Lake Railway could show an operational profit of $2,851,810 in the same year. In 1969 the line moved more than one million tons of freight, 75 per cent southbound, 25 per cent northbound. Mine produce made up 85 per cent of the southward movement, whereas 75 per cent of the freight going north represented petroleum products. The line had stimulated other mining along the route, as well as new forestry and farming, while 90,000 tons of material were delivered to the barge system at Hay River.

The origins of the White Pass and Yukon Railway were tied to the Klondike gold rush. Private investors took two years to construct a 110-mile (177 km) narrow gauge railway from Skagway, Alaska, to Whitehorse, Y.T., over a route which climbs 3000 ft (914 m) in the first 20 miles (32 km) and encounters extremes of cold and snow in winter. Operations began in 1900 and were linked first to river transportation subsidiaries and then to road activities in order to handle winter traffic on roads parallel to the frozen river, at which point a virtual monopoly had been established. Some mines developed their own roads connecting to the river transport and thence to the export facility of the railway, but an extension of the line to Mayo never materialized. Mining had become the the basis for the rail operation by 1914, but high transportation costs limited mining development and Rea (1968) suggests that a number of mines failed even prior to 1909 because of high transportation costs. The number of mines declined sharply in 1942, but traffic at that time went up to a record 300,000 tons in support of the construction of the Canol pipeline and the Alaska Highway. The railroad was leased to the U.S. army between 1942 and 1945. The track was improved, the rolling stock augmented, and a pipeline built along the right-of-way to handle the Canol production.

After 1945, traffic on the WPYR was driven up successively by production from the United Keno mines; Cassiar, Clinton Creek, Imperial mine-mill, and the Anvil mine at Faro and WPYR contracted with Anvil in 1969 to move 370,000 tons of concentrates every year to tidewater whence it is shipped to Japan.

The line has never received any subsidies or land grants, and it had a shaky financial history. It paid no dividends to investors for 48 years and over a large part of that time even failed to pay bond interest. The group at various times owned and operated trains, river steamers, horse drawn stages, an airline, trucks, tractors, and a pipeline.

Winter roads and the Alaska Highway, including its extensions to Dawson and Mayo, caused the abandonment of the river route in the 1950s, but the Company, which received badly needed refinancing from Britain in 1951, began to create a closely integrated modern system of transport services. The track was rebuilt and dieselized, a considerable expense since the locomotives were narrow gauge and built to unusual specifications. The tide terminus at Skagway had been served by three cargo ships of the Canadian Pacific Steamships and one Canadian National vessel, but in 1954 the WPYR organized yet another subsidiary, British Yukon Ocean Services Ltd., and began operations between Vancouver and Skagway, using the world's first vessel designed and built to operate as a container transport. The containers were one third of the 24 ft × 8 ft × 8 ft (7.3 × 2.4 × 2.4 m) standard size because of poor wharfing at Skagway, but the 4000 ton *Clifford Rogers* could handle 168 four-hundred-cubic-foot steel containers and 2500 tons of ore concentrates on standard pallets. Containers and pallets were handled by forklifts and they proved an immediate success. They offered shippers door-to-door service in sealed containers, almost eliminated losses and breakage in transit, and greatly reduced handling and paper work. The containers went on flat cars to Whitehorse where they were distributed to the interior by a trucking subsidiary. Success led to the construction of two larger vessels, hauling full-size containers to a rebuilt basin with wharves and storage capable of handling 4,000,000 tons a year. Straddle lifts for rapid handling and stowage of the units were installed at Vancouver and Skagway, and both heated and refrigerated containers provided for perishable goods. The final development in 1969, to cope with the Anvil contract, was the design and construction of the so-called 'teardrop' containers for ore concentrates, which could be hauled on the container flats of both truck and rail and then emptied safely and reliably in all weather conditions by standard lifts into bulk cargo space. The loading capacity off-rail to ship is 1500 tons an hour.

Outbound tonnage has increased from 100,000 tons per annum when containerization was introduced, to an assured 600,000 tons in 1972. The company expects more. Inbound freight, mainly food, manufactured goods, lumber, iron, cement, and steel, but including fuel through the pipeline, will total about 167,000 tons, so the imbalance in flow has been reversed.

Since modernization, the operations show a small but consistent profit, with most of it being put back as capital. As a result of containerization, profits have risen markedly. Rea (1968) shows the WPYR to be the most efficient of Canadian railways in the ratio of operating revenue to expense. Maintenance costs are 50 per cent higher than the national average, but operating costs are low because of the highly specialized equipment and integrated service, and net revenues exceed 6 per cent in most years. However, freight rates are high, 10.18 cents a ton/mile compared with a national average of 1.46 cents, and 7.16 cents per passenger mile compared with a national average of 2.87 cents. The high rates, however justified, are acknowledged by the company to have caused ill-will in the past, but this has changed as the route opened up development, and rates have been dropping steadily since 1955 in amounts ranging from 25 to 40 per cent. Furthermore, since the opening of the Highway, the group is no longer a monopoly. In addition, the high rates on the rail sector are offset by cheap ocean freight, so that combined costs for lead–zinc concentrates moving between Whitehorse and Vancouver have been estimated as low as 1.4 cents per ton/mile. The loss of cheap river transport has been clearly justified by the year-round capacity and versatility of trucking.

A transportation study for the federal government (Travacon Research Ltd. 1968) reviewed possible developments, including alternatives to the WPYR, but most alternatives involve astronomical construction costs, and it is still not possible to reach tidewater in Canada. The report concludes that the WPYR is adequate but that an extension might well be made to Ross River and the Anvil mine, which would also serve the larger community. It is suggested that it be narrow gauge for compatability, but that it be laid on standard gauge ties and roadbed to reduce the cost of upgrading the facility if freight demands continue to increase. There are also some rather remote proposals, with studies by DOT and CNR, of a Yukon–British Columbia railway joining the Pacific Great Eastern at Prince

George, and thence to the transcontinental net. The cost estimates are high and the benefits difficult to evaluate.

Road Transportation

The extent of the continuous road system is shown in Figure 3.6, together with the roads under construction, or proposed. Not shown are the many hundreds of short discontinuous roads serving mines, airstrips, and small communities isolated from the continuous system. Roads are extremely important, both because they serve as distributors for the bulk media at the operational level of occupation and development, and because they serve entire communities rather than single enterprises.

The government drew up a Northern Roads Policy in 1955, revised in 1961, which committed $10,000,000 a year to roads which would not merely serve immediate needs but also promote general access and both anticipate and encourage development.

Considering the area served, the highway system is limited, with some 600 miles (966 km) in the N.W.T. and perhaps 2500 miles (4023 km) in the Yukon. The Yukon net is more developed because of the Alaska Highway, 1220 miles (1963 km) of which lie within Canada, which provided land access to Yukon through Canada for the first time. Since the Highway was built solely to serve the airfields of the Northwest Staging Route, it is a good example of development following upon access, whatever the original purpose. A link to the sea at Haines soon followed, with improvements of the old winter roads to Mayo, Dawson, and then Keno Hill, with a Canol road to service the pipeline, and the Ross River–Cormacks road serving the Anvil mine. These roads are utilized by trucking, both from the railhead at Whitehorse, and overland from Dawson Creek, B.C. In addition to the normal distributive function of trucking, the entire mining economy of Yukon, with production exceeding 37 million dollars in 1969, depends upon the road system to get their product to the rail and the sea.

The Mackenzie roads build upon the Mackenzie Highway. It has been important in regional development and was used to help construction of the Great Slave Lake Railway.

It is difficult to find figures for passengers and freight over these roads, but one private company studying transportation requirements in 1960 became convinced that the greatest tonnage of all supplies entering the North went in trucks up the Alaska and Mackenzie highways.

The roads program is co-ordinated by the Northern Economic Development Branch of the Department of Indian Affairs and Northern Development. The territorial governments administer tote-trail subsidies

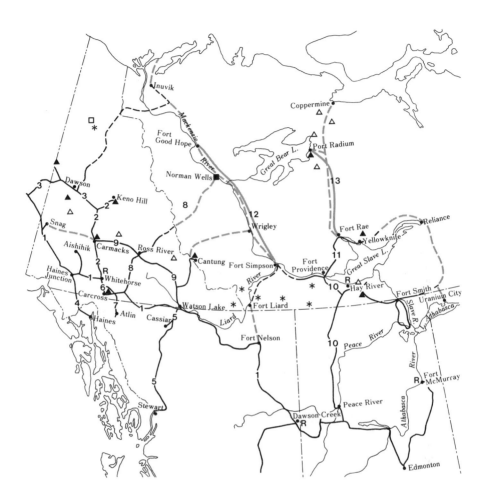

——	Existing road
- - -	Road under construction
━━	Major winter road
- - -	Possible future road
R	Railhead

▲	Producing mine area
△	Mine prospect
□	Oil well
■	Oil field
*	Gas well

1 Alaska Highway
2 Whitehorse-Keno Road
3 Stewart Crossing-Dawson-
   Alaska boundary (Clinton Creek)
4 Haines cut off
5 Watson Lake-(Cassiar)-Stewart
6 Tagish Road
7 Atlin Road

8 Canoe Road
9 Watson Lake-Carmacks Road
10 Mackenzie Highway
11 Fort Providence-Yellowknife Road
12 Winter toll road-Fort Good Hope.
   May extend to Inuvik
13 Fort Rae-Port Radium. Winter road
   with variations in route & tributaries

0   200 Miles
0   320 Kilometers

3.6
Northern Road System 1971

amounting to 50 per cent of the cost of roads to a minimal standard, giving temporary access to small mines, drill sites, fishing camps and such places, at costs of $5000 a mile or less. Maintained by the exploiter, they are kept open to the public. They include winter roads which depend upon packed snow surfaces and ice bridges over rivers and lakes. Most of these roads are temporary expedients and may be abandoned after serving their purpose, but if development occurs they may be improved and, if they meet highly specific standards, they may qualify for federal subsidies (*Prospectus: North of 60°* 1971). For example, a Permanent Access Road is defined as a high-standard all-weather gravel road not less than 24 ft (7.3 m) wide with curvatures less than 20° and gradients less than 10 per cent, and may receive subsidies up to two-thirds of a maximum $60,000 a mile. It must be maintained by the resource operator for public use. At the highest level the government itself builds and maintains roads designated as Resource Development Roads which serve several resources: Area Development Roads open up areas of potential productivity, and Communications Roads connect population centres. The terminology is inadequate since most such roads acquire multiple functions but they all have 32 ft (9.8 m) width between shoulders, maximum curvatures of 7° and maximum gradients of 5 per cent. All surfaces, bridges, and culverts can carry 90,000 lb (40,820 kg) loads, a continental standard. Such roads may average $100,000 a mile, with some sectors costing a great deal more in difficult terrain and maintenance is costly, even without considering the small volumes of traffic.

Vehicles using the roads are normal commercial types with normal equipment for cold and snow. Most trucking is by tractors and semi-trailers because of their versatility, including a quick turnaround for tractors to pre-loaded trailers, the ability to pass the Alaska Highway in bond with different hauliers, and the ability to piggyback the trailers on rail and barge. Furthermore, the modern truck has astonishing off-road capability. Containerization has begun, but still on flat-bed semi-trailers. It is more advanced in the Yukon because of the activities of the White Pass and Yukon Corporation, but NTC has modified some barges for deck-loading containers and they are entering the N.W.T.

The ton/mile cost on improved roads is given as 8 cents by Weick and Merrill (1969), but in practice rates vary considerably. The *Prospectus: North of 60°* quotes rates between Edmonton and Hay River at $4.22 per cwt for meat, $3.75 per cwt for vegetables, and $2.52 per cwt for roofing supplies. The cost of moving ore in the Yukon is less, and a great deal depends upon reliability of the traffic in terms of tonnage, timing, and type.

Winter roads, in use since the last century, are now being developed and used more widely (Wonders 1962). While the seasonal restriction is a severe economic handicap, the low cost and maintenance figures, combined with the ability of modern trucks to use the roads without modification, is extremely attractive. The Arctic Transportation Study gives $500 per mile as a general cost and maintenance figure, but one company opened and maintained 500 miles (805 km) of snow road out of Fort Rae, N.W.T., for less than $120 a mile in 1970.

Rivers and lakes provide bridges and level roads when frozen, usually by mid-November, and remain serviceable until about mid-April. The ATS, assuming tonnages of 20,000 per annum over a 300-mile (481 km) snow road estimates ton/mile costs of 6 cents, but experience suggests that 20 cents is more realistic. For example, when the ATS assumes an annual vehicle tonnage of 4000 in 90-ton loads, the reality for the company quoted above was 280 tons per vehicle in 35–40 ton loads. Speeds on another road average 16 m.p.h. (26 km p.h.) rather than the assumed 25 (40 km p.h.) in the ATS.

In 1970/1 Western Electronics and Engineering opened a winter toll road 480 miles (773 km) down the Mackenzie from Fort Simpson to Fort Good Hope. It may be extended to Inuvik, a total of 735 miles (1183 km). Intended mainly for drilling and geophysical studies it also took in traffic for pipe-line studies, and demonstrated the access concept by delivering supplies to communities along a route which had never seen a road vehicle. Again suboptimal traffic meant high costs since the toll alone was 4 cents a ton/mile on the gross vehicle weight.

Non-Conventional Vehicles for Northern Transportation
A variety of unconventional and undeveloped transport modes have been discussed. They include nuclear submarine freighters, capsule and 'solid' pipelines, air-cushion vehicles (ACVs), greatly enlarged STOL and VTOL craft, further development of high capacity trucks, and a variety of off-road vehicles with exotic modes of propulsion. There is an extensive literature of this latter group but they are almost certainly not economically viable.

There are a number of highly developed over-snow vehicles. The best known is Bombardier's Snowmobile with a 60 m.p.h. (97 km p.h.) capability and a 3000 lb (1361 kg) payload, but there is a range of exceptionally reliable and capable cargo carriers made by Nodwell of Calgary which have been successful over snow and muskeg with up to 27000 lb (12,250 kg) payloads and modest operating costs. Alone among the specialized vehicles their payload exceeds vehicle weight, and their ground pressures are all 2 lb/sq in. (0.9 kg/6.4 cm²) or less.

ACVs have been tested and performed well in the North, beginning with a Saunders-Roe SRN4 in 1966 and an SRN6 in 1968. They were fully amphibious with flexible 'skirts' that can clear obstacles 75 per cent of skirt height. They climb steady gradients of 1 in 8, short grades of 1:3. Variations include a marine ACV with rigid side walls and flexible front and rear curtains, which may be driven by a water screw, offers better control, and reduces operating costs by half, but cannot operate over land or ice. An 'off-road' ACV has its weight sustained by an air-cushion but has powered wheels for traction and control, giving high off-road capacity with good control and good climbing ability. At a level of minimum versatility is the tracked ACV in which the vehicle uses a prepared track to gain high safe speeds and optimal operating conditions. There are plans for 4000-ton ACVs and experiments aimed at providing more efficient curtains and reducing the power/weight ratio of 100 h.p./ton which gives high fuel consumptions at present. The expensive aero engines now in use are not really necessary when considered in terms of safety. It has been proposed that strings of hoverbarges could be towed over suitable routes, e.g. the Mackenzie River, summer and winter, at 30 m.p.h. (48 km p.h.) or more. These hoverbarges could cross land, and being articulated, would conform to the microrelief with a saving in power and fuel consumption.

An SRN4 cost 4½ million dollars in 1969 and could travel at 70 m.p.h. (113 km p.h.) with a 60-ton payload. Ton/mile cost for an annual utilization of 2000 hours is 74 cents while an SRN6 costing $350,000 and capable of 60 m.p.h. (97 km p.h.) with a 3-ton payload, would give $1.96 per ton/mile. Optimal conditions might halve these rates but they still compare unfavourably with aircraft. Unless there are improvements in DOC, they may well be confined to operations using its special abilities, for example lightering of freight.

At many places in the Canadian Arctic, freight is handled from the ship to a lighter, from the lighter to the beach, and from the beach to a warehouse, with handling costs running as high as $45 a ton. The ACV could cross water, ice, and the beach to the warehouse, eliminating capital equipment on the beach. It would save time because of its speed and so extend the range of the mother ship and, by crossing fringing ice along the shore, it could extend the shipping season.

Conveyor belts have been suggested for the movement of minerals. They have low man power requirements and can be sheltered from the environment, but they demand a consistent supply of freight for economic operation. The technology is well understood and Warnock Hersey's estimate (1970) for 5½ mile (9 km) belts with a vertical lift of 130 feet (40

m) and annual tonnage of 3½ million provides a range from 5.8 cents per ton/mile to 6.4 cents per ton/mile for three types. Ore may be discharged to another belt for greater mileages.

Nuclear powered freighter submarines have been suggested for bulk transport. They would cruise at 400 ft (122 m) and require 150 or 200 ft (46 or 61 m) of water in order to approach a harbour under ice. Consequently, the number of suitable sites is very limited, but docking areas can be kept clear of ice by air-bubbling systems. Large hatches are undesirable and the most suitable freight would be ore or oil; hence vessels of 250,000 DWT have been proposed, 1000 ft (305 m) long with a beam of 180 ft (55 m) and a height from keel to sail of about 100 ft (30 m). The minimum operating draught, 60 ft (18 m), would be when surfaced. They would navigate with the aid of a VLF radio system, and civilian sonar and echo sounders to measure ice draft are available. There is a need to take up ballast water when discharging and the rate of discharge or loading would need to be 16,000 tons an hour in order to achieve a 24-hour turnaround. This is possible with present technology. Such a tanker might cost $135,000,000, and could operate over a 5000 mile (8047 km) route with a DOC of about 0.126 cents per ton/mile, a cost second only to standard pipeline in the south. Most authorities are sceptical about realizing such low rates during the pioneer development, and insurance costs might be prohibitive. There is little likelihood of such a vessel being built in the immediate future.

Pipelines

Oil and gas pipelines were being considered during 1971 to handle the potential production of northern oil and gas. The Prudhoe Bay discoveries in Alaska stimulated an international debate about the route for a 48 in. (1219 mm) pipeline. A route across the Brooks Range and south to Valdez, Alaska, is the shortest in spite of technical problems, but the ocean haul from Valdez to the American northwest is considered to provide an environmental hazard, and is being contested by conservationists. An alternative route, which would also handle Canadian oil and link with the existing North American pipeline system, has been proposed for the Mackenzie Valley.

There is prior experience with Canol, a 580-mile (933 km) pipeline completed in 1944 by U.S. Army engineers to connect the oil field at Norman Wells to a refinery of strategic importance at Whitehorse, Y.T. Production at Norman Wells rose from 267,000 barrels in 1943 to 1,250,000 in 1944 but fell back to 353,000 the following year, and the end of the war emergency caused Norman Wells to revert to its role as a local producer. Rea (1968) quotes this as an example of economics rather than technology governing northern development, since this line which, together with a pipeline down the White Pass and Yukon Railway linked the field to tidewater and the outside market, never operated as an export facility. In fact the WPYR operated their section not for the export of Norman Wells oil refined at Whitehorse, but for the import of refined products to Whitehorse from the U.S. Pacific coast, the delivered product being cheaper. In view of a million dollar annual maintenance cost the Canol line and its road were closed, although the road was later reopened as far as Ross River and is important for mining.

Conservationists have been concerned about the construction of pipelines in the Arctic because of the danger that oil, heated to make it flow, would melt the permafrost and begin permanent damage at the surface. Pipelines may be buried; laid on a gravel embankment or suspended above the surface. If laid on the surface or above, it would be difficult to move oil in winter unless the lines were both insulated and heated. Buried line would not be subject to temperature changes, but burying a 48 in. (1219 mm) pipe in an 8 ft (2.4 m) trench in permafrost would be difficult and expensive, the danger of melting the permafrost and disrupting the pipe would be high, and the cost of adequate insulation might be prohibitive. The most satisfactory protection is to suspend the line, but a 48 in. (1219 mm) pipeline which carries 35 tons of oil in each 100 ft (30 m) of pipe would need strong supports. In 1970 and 1971 a consortium called Mackenzie Valley Pipeline Research Ltd. was conducting a study to show the physical and economic feasibility of a 48 in (1219 mm) pipe-pine from Alaska to Edmonton via the Mackenzie Valley and they were operating a short section of pipe the year around at Inuvik.

Pipelines are best laid across muskeg when it is frozen, but mid-winter conditions may be too severe, so that laying may be restricted to the spring unless there is an abundant supply of gravel when summer work becomes feasible. A pipe-laying crew requires 500 to 700 men, a logistic problem in remote areas, and transport for pipeline is also difficult. The needs for a Prudhoe Bay–Valdez pipeline were estimated at 80,000 joints of pipe.

The logistics suggest that a routeway such as the Mackenzie is to be preferred since cheap transportation by barge is available and a route could be chosen which would avoid muskeg and soils with a high ice content. During the closed period on the river, winter roads could serve to redistribute the pipe from storage sites.

It has been suggested that oil from the Arctic Island could best be handled on the first part of the journey by submarine pipelines, based upon experience with PLUTO (Pipeline under the ocean) across the English Channel during the Normandy invasion of 1944, when 4.8 in. (122 mm) ID pipe was used to transport fuel. Flexible pipe, 8 in. (203 mm), is now technically possible and could be laid in multiples to handle the necessary volumes. A series of routes from Banks Island were surveyed in 1969 and four specific channels recommended.

There could be pipelines from various island sites to a suitable terminal for year-round operations by submarines, or surface tankers during the open season, possibly in short hauls to an *entrepôt* at a permanently open port. This, however, involves expensive storage facilities.

Gas may also be piped and Panarctic made a major gas find on King Christian Island in 1969. Demand is increasing and gas pipelines appeal to conservationists since gas flows at ambient temperatures and the permafrost would not be threatened.

Costs for northern construction of pipeline are very high. The estimate for a Trans-Alaska pipeline is $1,000,000 per mile for 800 miles (1288 km) of 48 in. (1219 mm) pipe. A 42 in. (1067 mm) line over a less rugged route down the Mackenzie would cost $375,000 per mile. Operating costs are expected to be higher in the Arctic since cold oil will need more energy to pump or fuel to heat, and the insulation of pipe would increase capital costs. A 1970 estimate by Warnock Hersey for 42 in. (1067 mm) and 48 in. (1219 mm) pipelines, 1500 miles (2414 km) long, with an annual throughput of 12.3 million tons show red DOCs of 0.068 cents per ton/mile, but there is a considerable saving in amortization and interest costs through using a 42 in. (1067 mm) pipe rather than 48 in. (1219 mm), with total costs of 0.284 cents and 0.765 cents per ton/mile respectively.

Conclusions

Events of the last 20 years in the Canadian North demonstrate that there are no technical limitations upon transportation. The real problem lies in moving materials at costs low enough to allow northern residents a competitive place in the national economy and access to external markets.

In developed areas there exists a hierarchy of systems capable of dealing with every phase of demands, varying greatly in size, type, and duration, with all systems having access to a complex transcontinental network, the costs of which are shared by the total community. The location of industries sensitive to transportation costs may be decided by centfractional differences in the cost of a service, rather than by whether service is available at all; and adequate transportation for associated activities and labour can usually be assumed.

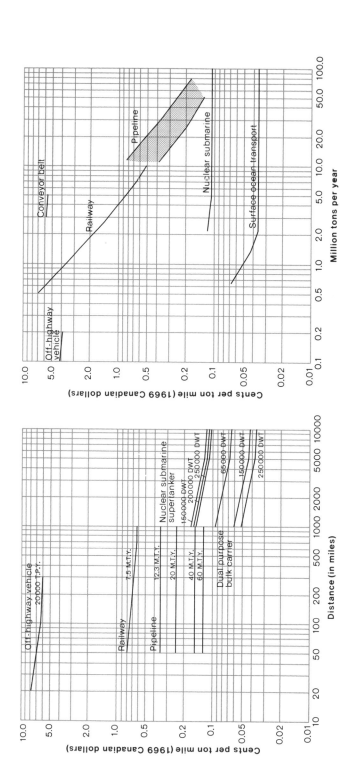

3.7

Costs of Transportation as a Function of Distance

(Source: Arctic Transportation Study 1970)

3.8

Costs of Transportation as a Function of Yearly Quantity

(Source: Arctic Transportation Study 1970)

This is not true in the North. The majority of communities may depend upon a single transportation type, and the requirements of both the operator and the user emphasize versatility of the medium rather than minimal cost of operation. Yet each mode is heavily dependent upon operating within certain tonnages and distances for efficiency (Figures 3.7 and 3.8), so that it is difficult to identify examples of optimal utilization of any system in the North. Versatility, seasonal traffic, one-way hauls, and single commodity production of small communities help explain why traffic flows do not attain the thresholds required by more efficient, lower operating cost systems. Also there were formerly many examples of operators using out-of-date inefficient media for short-term projects to avoid capital investment.

Interest charges and amortization of facilities can double or triple the effective ton/mile costs for short-term projects, and most mineral production has a limited life. Yet the installation of high capacity systems has usually depended upon single enterprises. Even such a vast resource as the Pine Point lead and zinc deposits failed to induce the owners to invest the considerable capital required to establish a well-proven means of transport, the railway, while investors willing to experiment with facilities of more appropriate function like the *Manhattan* tanker project and the Mackenzie Pipeline feasibility study have been rare.

The capital costs involved may run to hundreds of millions of dollars, and while cost-benefit analyses may or may not show substantial benefits for the area as a whole (as of 1971 there was no such documented study), there is no doubt that similar sums invested in a developed area would produce greater returns with less effort and risk.

It is necessary to distinguish between what may be possible and what is actually done. Government administrators and producers choose from the means available and there have been many unpublished practical studies selecting the cheapest and most effective 'mix.' Few are published. The reality they describe is limited in capacity and expensive, with all costs higher than those in the South by amounts ranging from 20 to 500 per cent. Different assumptions give varying figures but in one account, 1969 costs were described as follows (Table 3.1).

Even when ton/mile costs appear acceptably low, the great distances can mean real costs, e.g. $200 a ton, for Dewline supplies to a remote Arctic beach in 1958, and $73 a ton for ore shipped by air from the Barrens to Winnipeg – figures remote indeed from estimates like $1.95 per ton for Mackenzie oil to the u.s. East Coast, $5.28 per ton for the same oil by pipeline to Edmonton (Arctic Transportation Study 1970).

The greater number of studies (Battelle Memorial Institute 1961; Travacon Research Ltd. 1968; and Warnock Hersey International 1970) are aimed at ways of utilizing potential resources through systems yet to be developed, and though possibly accurate as cost estimates, are highly speculative as to which resources will, in fact, be utilized and as to where the capital will be found. It is difficult to forecast how and when the relevant decisions will be made, although something must be done about oil in the near future.

Governmental policies are clearly designed to bridge the gap between the present reality and adequate future means. There is a declared belief in regional access, a systematic long-term commitment to the construction of roads, airfields, and navigational aids, and established subsidies for similar facilities used in private development. There is also a demonstrated willingness to provide capital for such major projects as the Great Slave Lake Railway. These policies rest on the belief that while serving essentially one resource at the outset, such facilities finally serve a larger and enlarging community while providing the essential base upon which subsidiary systems may build, ultimately providing carrier services comparable to those enjoyed by the country as a whole.

4 Mining in the Canadian North

GEORGE TOUGH

During 1970, there were about 240 mines in operation in Canada, most of them in mid-northern or far northern regions. In addition, there were numerous oil and gas wells, nearly all of which were in the plains of Alberta, Saskatchewan, and Manitoba.[1] From these scattered sources, whose locations are shown in Figure 4.1, came production valued at some $5.8 billion in 1970. The benefit to the national economy was considerable: the mineral industry component makes up about 7 per cent of the Gross National Product. Nationally, about 110,000, or 2 per cent of the total labour force, were employed in mining in 1968. In addition, demands by the industry for capital equipment, supplies, and services generate substantial employment, much of it in the industrial heartland of settled Canada.

In recent years a spirited debate has developed in Canada concerning the benefits derived from the mining industry. On the one hand there are those who argue that the capital intensity of the industry is so pronounced, and increasing to such a degree, that it offers few employment opportunities with increasing production. As supports for this view it is pointed out that from 1957 to 1967, the value of production from mines rose from $1.7 billion to $3.2 billion, some 87 per cent, while estimated direct employment in mining rose only from 101,132 to 102,680 (Statistics Canada 1961–8). Attention is called as well to problems inherent in economies dependent on exhaustible resources. Between 1957 and 1967, 82 metal mines closed in Canada, or nearly 45 per cent of all the metal mines operating in 1957. Critics point also to the low level of public revenues accruing from the mineral industry in the form of corporate income taxes. In 1968, for example, the industry paid Federal income taxes amounting to about $90 million from a book profit of approximately $755 million (Can-

1 Oil and gas production receives cursory attention in this paper, since it is only recently that attention has been focused on oil and gas in the North. Sand and gravel and similar operations are excluded from discussion.

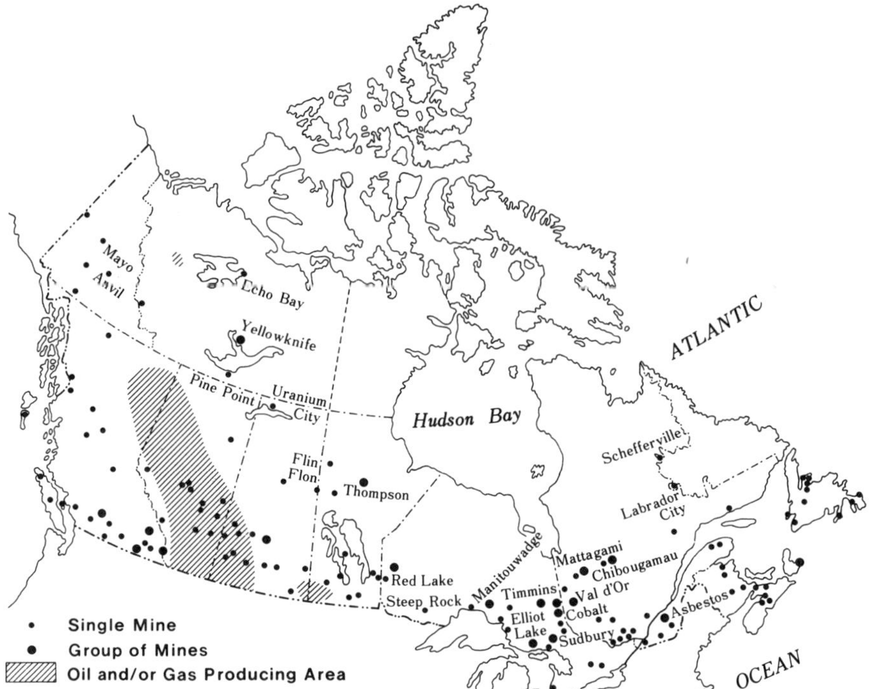

Mayo
Anvil
Echo Bay
Yellowknife
Pine Point
Uranium City
Hudson Bay
Flin Flon
Thompson
Red Lake
Steep Rock
Manitouwadge
Timmins
Elliot Lake
Cobalt
Sudbury
Mattagami
Chibougamau
Val d'Or
Asbestos
Schefferville
Labrador City
ATLANTIC
OCEAN
Single Mine
Group of Mines
Oil and/or Gas Producing Area

4.1

Mining Operations in Canada, 1970

(Source: Dept. of Energy, Mines and Resources.
Map 900A: Principal Mineral Areas of Canada, 1970)

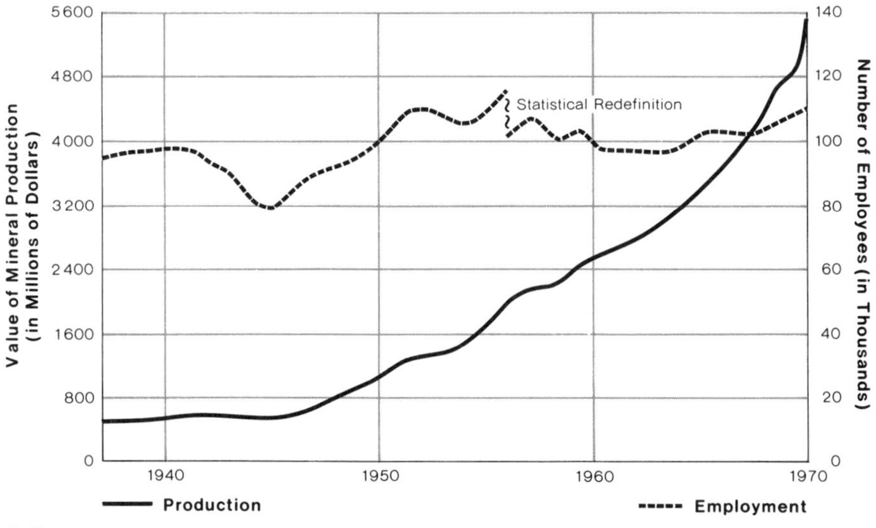

Value of Mineral Production (in Millions of Dollars)
0
800
1600
2400
3200
4000
4800
5600
Number of Employees (in Thousands)
0
20
40
60
80
100
120
140
1940
1950
1960
1970
Statistical Redefinition
Production
Employment

4.2

Production and Employment in the Mining Industry, 1937-1970

(Source: D.B.S., General Review of the Mining Industry)

ada Dept. Nat. Rev. 1971, p. 49). Moreover, the federal government paid out, to the gold and coal mining industries alone, direct subsidies amounting to some $52.7 million in the same year (Canada Dept. Finance 1968, pp. 10, 24–36). Finally, the increasing dominance of the industry by non-Canadians is a source of concern. Between 1965 and 1967, the proportion of the mining industry controlled by outsiders rose from 64.4 per cent to 71 per cent; the implications for resource policy call for some anxiety.

The counter-arguments have been strongly presented too. The contribution to national revenue has already been pointed out, and proponents emphasize the multiplier effect on income and employment in Canada. Some have suggested that nearly 20 per cent of the Canadian labour force derives its livelihood indirectly from the industry, and considerable change in the settlement pattern and growth of transport networks has been the direct result of new mines coming into production in response to increasing mineral demands. In addition, much is made of the fact that indigenous supplies of essential raw materials are provided for Canadian industries, while export revenues contribute in a major way to our balance of payments on merchandise account. Nearly 60 per cent of Canadian production is exported; mineral exports constitute some 28 per cent of these total Canadian exports. As proof of the dynamism of the mineral sector, it is pointed out that, while 82 mines closed in the decade 1957–67, 102 mines opened (Figure 4.3), many of which were in proximity to worked-out mines and provided continuing community support and new opportunities for displaced miners. It is argued that without the incentives provided by liberal taxation policies, many of these new mines would not have been brought into production. Finally, it is evident that outside the major manufacturing regions in the southern fringe of the country, there is heavy dependence on the industry and that dependence is deceptively hidden in the national data usually used in the debate. Whereas mining employs only 2 per cent of Canada's labour force, the proportion rises significantly as one moves north, reaching over 50 per cent in some districts.

It is the latter point that must be brought out in any discussion of the North, for it is evident from Figure 4.1 that, notwithstanding the leakage of benefits to the heartland and to non-Canadians from exploitation of northern mineral resources, mining has been and will remain a major economic keystone in the North. Numerous cities such as Sudbury, Ontario (1966 population 84,888) and Noranda, Quebec (11,521) depend heavily on local mineral industries for their economic support; for smaller centres such as Schefferville, Elliot Lake, or Uranium City the existence of a mineral complex is the only reason for their creation and survival.

Temporal–Spatial Development

Spatial development of the Canadian mining industry has been shaped largely by private corporate decisions, influenced to some degree by public policies. It is only of comparatively recent date that governments have attempted actively to affect the thrust of exploration and exploitation. Examples of this new approach include the federal Roads to Resources Program, Northern Mineral Exploration Grants, and federal government participation in the Panarctic Oils consortium. Canadian policy in general has been to maintain a uniformly liberal environment, letting physical and commercial factors determine the rate and location of mineral industry developments.

Exploitation of a mineral deposit, once discovered, is determined by relationships among these general factors: demand for the mineral as expressed in its price, cost of access and transportation, the unit value of the mineral product, and the cost involved in bringing it to the shipping stage. Accordingly, it is not surprising that the first major mining ventures in Canada, in the eighteenth century, were simple operations, exploiting coal and iron ore for predominantly local use, in the Maritimes and in the St Lawrence Valley. Extensions into the interior occurred where high-value ore bodies, such as the copper deposits near Bruce Mines on Lake Huron, were located close to low-cost transport. With improvements in both transportation and mining technology, other deposits in the then 'developed' areas of Canada were opened up – the iron mines near Marmora were in operation in the early 1800s and several small mines exploiting base metals were operating in the Eastern Townships of Quebec and Nova Scotia. In 1866, gold was discovered near Madoc, Ontario, the first such discovery in the Canadian Shield. Although this deposit proved of little commercial significance, it was a harbinger of the future role of the Shield's gold in Canadian mining, and of its contribution to Canadian mineral development. As the nineteenth century approached, considerable development had taken place along this eastern access corridor, although the Canadian Shield had scarcely been penetrated.

The construction of the CPR north and west from the lowlands through the Canadian Shield was a major cost reducer for Northern Ontario locations, and a fortuitous discovery near Sudbury, Ontario, during construction of the line initiated activity that was to eventuate in what is now the most important single nickel–copper producing area in North America. As the CPR traversed the Prairies and penetrated the western mountain barrier, it gave access to major coal reserves, to base metal deposits of lesser significance, and to many smaller deposits all along its route.

Meanwhile, access by sea had prompted considerable prospecting and

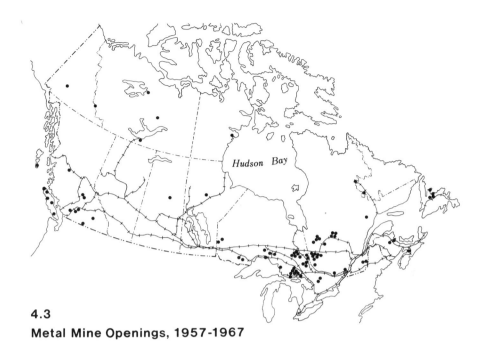

4.3

Metal Mine Openings, 1957-1967

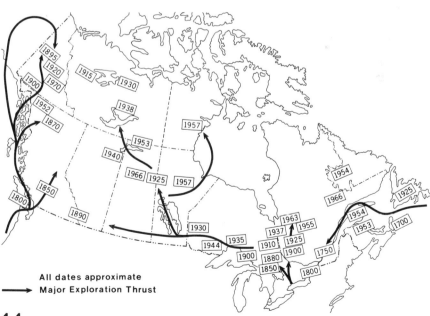

All dates approximate
→ Major Exploration Thrust

4.4

Selected Mining Developments: Date of First Production

development of coal and, later, gold in British Columbia. Intermittent coal mining commenced about 1840 on Vancouver Island, and first reports of placer gold were received in 1855. Immediately, local prospectors were joined by a throng of gold-seekers spreading north from the u.s. gold fields. The major rivers were soon ascended, with shortlived camps springing up well into the interior of the region. Some prospectors bypassed these fields to investigate the river valleys of Alaska and the Yukon. This search was rewarded in 1896 by the discovery of major placer gold deposits at Dawson City on the Yukon River. By the end of 1900, gold valued at more than $50 million had been washed out of the river valleys of this small region. However, this level of output could not be sustained; production fell to an average of $5 million yearly by 1906-15.

These gold discoveries were soon followed by major silver and gold finds in the eastern Canadian north as the next stage of railroad building, designed to open up agricultural lands in the Canadian Shield, provided access to the Cobalt, Timmins, and Kirkland Lake areas. These developments were followed in turn by discoveries in northwestern Quebec.

By 1930 the Canadian mid-North had undergone the first 'skimming' process: only those deposits that were readily discoverable were found, and only those materials of high unit value were exploited. Two processes have continued in the North since these early incursions by prospectors: forays into isolated areas to develop high-value discoveries such as gold, radium and uranium, or the silver–lead ores of the Mayo district in the Yukon, and the more painstaking development, dependent on improved access or technical innovation, of lower-value deposits such as the Pine Point lead–zinc ores in the Great Slave Lake area. To a degree Figure 4.4 illustrates this phenomenon as well as the major thrusts acting upon the North. The pattern of spatial development has not been an orderly one: dots have appeared and vanished on the map of northern Canada, individual mines have given rise to new communities, seldom followed by lasting economic activity and settlement. In general, it has been the less glamorous minerals – nickel, copper, iron ore – that provided the long-term basis for viable regional development. This is due in no small measure to the constraints imposed by high unit costs of production: exploitation of lower-value goods is usually more dependent on the steady improvement of exploration, mining, and metallurgical technology, or of transport facilities on a large-scale, than on the ease of mineral discovery. However, it is well known that many of today's base metal and iron mines were first discovered by prospectors seeking precious metals. In this respect gold has played a key role beyond its contribution to general economic development.

Spatial aspects aside, the past few decades have witnessed important changes in the industry itself, with meaningful implications for the national economy and, to a greater degree, for the regions in which mining plays a dominant role.

Owing to technological advances, ore of lower quality is being successfully mined each year. Figure 4.5 shows this both nationally and for the Northwest Territories; the contrasts prevailing in a remote area where intermittent skimming of high-grade deposits produces widely fluctuating relationships may be observed.

The general improvement in mineral resource conservation is not an unmixed blessing, since increasing proportions of waste rock have a proportionally increased impact on the local environment, and milling technology continues to require finer grinding and more complex chemical processes, both of which bring added problems in water and soil pollution. Finally, the per unit demand for energy is growing, and the development of further energy sources creates further problems.

Much of this technological change has resulted in decreased manpower needs. In terms of real-dollar output per employee the industry's production has risen from $11,147 in 1950 to $35,475 in 1967. Whereas, in 1950, wages and salaries were 30 per cent of production value, they were only 15 per cent of this value in 1967. In 1950, only 2 per cent of Canadian metal mines were open pit operations, but 20 per cent were of this type in 1968. This is causing not only diminished labour inputs but changing occupational requirements as well. One result is that labour mobility in the North between, for example, a depleted gold mine and an open-pit iron mine is inhibited, especially in the case of older miners, with some ensuing dislocation in areas where closures have been concentrated.

Mining in the North Today
Canada has often been described as a semi-industrialized nation, with its chief international role being a supplier of resource for the more advanced economies of the world. Whatever the extent to which this is so, the North is an exaggerated Canada – in effect, a subcolony of the North American industrial scene, and dependent on the world's need for minerals and on the decisions of large corporations based in Toronto, New York, London, or Tokyo. One implication of this is that, to an increasing degree, the Canadian North is in competition with mineral-rich areas all over the world, and capital derived from the North's mineral resources may be respent less and less in the region by mining corporations developing new ore bodies.

The principal resources providing economic support for the North are forest products and minerals. Other resources such as furs, fish, and agricultural products are less important in the aggregate (and are declining) although they remain crucial to some smaller northern centres. The scenic and game resources are becoming increasingly valuable for a growing tourist industry.

Mining developments in the North have two main roles: in virgin territory new mines serve to stimulate transportation and power network extensions, the movement of manpower, and the creation of new townsites. In occupied areas, the advent of mining operations can provide a diversified economic base for the region. Depending on their scale and duration, these operations can stimulate both backward and forward linkages – local fabrication of mining equipment, or a smelter – refinery complex, for example. Development theory contends that through time the importance of the original mining base will diminish as more advanced industry comes in. However, current reality indicates that the same transport improvements which facilitated economic shipment of mineral resources from the North has removed most of the rationale for local manufacturing (or agricultural) industries to serve either the mine or its dependent community. Similarly, forward linkages are inhibited not only by the preferences of metal customers but by cost considerations that favour locations removed from isolated mining centres. An excellent example of this program is the Pine Point mine which has ample reserves to warrant construction of a local smelter. The firm argued that a smelter at that location would be non-competitive, and was successful in obtaining permission to export the mineral in concentrate form. In fact, there are several cases where local forward linkages came about only after government action in the form of either persuasion or financial incentive. At Timmins, Ontario, the zinc refinery now under construction provides the latest example of a government desire to reduce the dependence of mining communities on strictly local deposits of non-renewable resources, and to provide a long-term stable economic base.

Within this huge region, it is possible to examine at one time the several stages through which mining districts pass in the North, and by case selection, we can examine some of the characteristics of the region's mineral economy and the communities it supports.

The New Quebec–Labrador iron area comprises the town of Schefferville and Labrador City, and could be stretched to include Gagnon, 100 miles (161 km) to the south. From the mines of this district, which opened up in the mid 1950s, comes over 70 per cent of Canada's iron ore, most of it for export to the u.s. and other foreign markets. In this region can be seen on a massive scale the type of open-pit operations required to extract

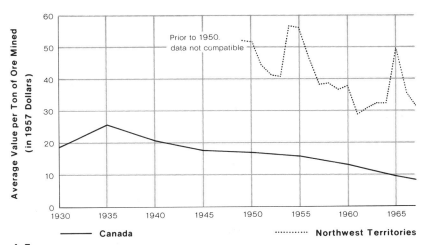

4.5

Average Ore Values, Canada and Northwest Territories, 1930-1967

(Source: D.B.S., General Review of the Mining Industry)

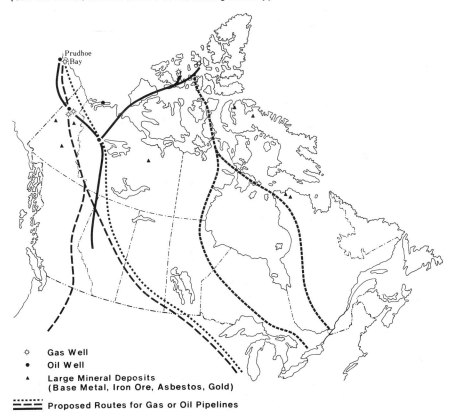

4.6

Potential Mineral Developments in the North

low unit value materials in a harsh environment. Considerable adaptation in mining processes and equipment was necessitated by environmental conditions. However, a visitor to the townsite sees little adaptation in the modes of townsite layout or in building construction: the neat detached houses, the winding crescents, the shopping plazas, could all be part of any city in southern Canada. Housing standards are rigorously enforced by company–municipal policies, and one sees no shacks in Labrador City. Recently announced expansion of mining and treatment facilities will add to the national contribution of this district and to its long-term viability.

The Ontario–Quebec gold belt provides a major contrast. This half-century old district, originally based on gold mining, forestry, and Clay-Belt farming, has seen its gold mines close at an accelerating rate, until now there remain only twelve, employing about 4500 men. In 1951, more than 13,500 men were working in the area's gold mines. Other mines, most notably the Noranda, Quemont, and Normetal copper operations, the Adams iron mine, and most recently the Ecstall base metal development, provide economic support for the communities, and, to a lesser extent, opportunities for displaced gold miners. However, expected mine closures over the next few years will mean that new mines, especially today's capital intensive type, will not be able to take up the slack. Trends in other basic sectors are also negative, especially in agriculture – in Abitibi County the farm population fell from 38,627 in 1951 to 19,189 in 1966; of the farmers remaining, the majority worked off the farm for much of the year. The recent road blockade set up in the district was a forceful demonstration of the plight of a region which had come to depend on mining and which has witnessed depletion of its minerals. The future of such a region is uncertain: there is continuing support for economic activity in the region, but at a reduced scale. Government aid for the region has had four main facets. Federal assistance to the region's gold mines has totalled nearly $200 million since 1948, and has retarded the decline of dependent communities. It has also bought time to discover new non-gold mines in the area, and considerable success, some of it shortlived, has resulted. In addition, the area is designated under the Regional Development Incentives Act. To date there has been little success, with the exception of the base metal processing facilities in Timmins and Noranda, both now under construction. Provincial action has taken the form of expanded educational and health facilities, which have had the side-benefit of providing considerable local employment. However, careful planning is necessary in such cases to ensure efficient utilization of these facilities, especially when regional populations are either static or declining. More recently, both provinces have taken action through regional exploration grants and other mechanisms to bring new mines to the area.

One of the main disappointments has been the lack of backward linkages that have developed; a recent study in the region indicated that, with minor exceptions, all of the capital and operating equipment and supplies originated outside the district, despite over 60 years of mining activity. This district, together with the nearby Cobalt silver area, epitomizes the problems inherent in long-term dependence on a wasting resource, and demonstrates that in Canada we are still much more adept at opening up areas than we are at keeping them open on a lasting viable basis.

The Sudbury district is perhaps the best known of all Canadian mineral producing regions. From the rocks of this basin comes about one-half of the non-Communist world's nickel, and large quantities of copper, gold, platinum, and other minerals. In normal times the area is short of suitable manpower and serves as a magnet for men from all parts of the North and the Atlantic Provinces. A large portion of the funds expended by the federal government under the Manpower Mobility Program is devoted to transferring men here. The stability of Sudbury has been promoted not only by its vast ore reserves, but also by the near-monopolistic position enjoyed by the area's nickel producers.

The Elliot Lake District, 100 miles (161 km) to the west, exemplifies a real problem in planning resource towns in the North. In the early 1950s, there was great demand in the United States and the United Kingdom for uranium, principally for defence purposes. Major discoveries in the Elliot Lake area soon resulted in mining operations, and with high prices and assured markets, twelve mines were operating at the peak of activity. From the outset there was concern that the resulting community be properly planned and constructed, and government agencies played a major role in the development of this new model northern town.

At the end of 1959, uranium buyers realized that sufficient uranium had been contracted to meet foreseeable requirements. Most options to continue purchases beyond 1963 were dropped, although stretched-out delivery schedules eased the impact somewhat. The United States had in the interim encouraged domestic production of uranium to such an extent that it is at present self-sufficient in that field. The result is that today there are only two producing companies at Elliot Lake, and over $100 million in public funds has been allocated to date in a stockpiling program designed to maintain the community until the revival of markets. Indications are that by the mid 1970s there will be sufficient commercial demand to maintain the area's mines. The short history of Elliot Lake mirrors that of numerous mining centres in the North, but it is of particular interest because it is an excellent example of flawed resource-town planning, which seems to have paid considerable attention to buildings and infrastructure, and less attention to the resource base of the community.

Further north and west in Ontario, the major centres are Wawa, where iron mining has been carried on since 1899, Steep Rock, where the only non-affiliated iron mine in Canada is located, and the Red Lake area, where gold mining has to an increasing degree been supplemented by iron and base metal mining. Red Lake has experienced considerable growth in its tourist industry, serving principally as a jumping-off point for U.S. hunters and fishermen.

Two districts dominate the Manitoba mineral economy. Flin Flon is the older, with its base metal mine, smelter and refinery starting operations in 1930. The company has pursued an aggressive exploration policy in the surrounding area, and has succeeded in locating new mines to maintain smelter feed. The town, with a population of 10,201 in 1966, has maintained a marked degree of stability, and presents an opportunity to examine the local employment impact of a mineral complex. In 1961, total employment at the local mines and processing facilities, was 54 per cent of the total local labour force. This community has been used as a yardstick in several studies relating to the effects of new long-term mining ventures in a remote area.

Thompson, with it fully integrated nickel complex, owes its origin to the new style exploration program characteristic of powerful mining firms that are increasingly dominating the northern scene. Geophysics played a principal role in the discovery of these ore bodies, and large sums were spent on exploratory drilling and development work after specific targets were selected in the broad region of interest, which lies along a major fault zone trending northeast through Manitoba.

A modern community has resulted, and from the beginning rigid controls on subdivisions and building construction have prevailed. However, this resulted in the creation of an unofficial satellite community nearby, populated largely by Indians who are not involved beneficially in the activity stemming from the advent of the new mine. The benefits from mining activity to the Indians at Thompson, as in much of the North, have been minimal, despite the apparently paradoxical situation that sees extremely high labour turnover at the mines, and few real attempts to utilize local Indians as mine workers. The record of the industry so far, with few exceptions, is summed up in the one word 'unsatisfactory,' but until recently government has not given explicit attention to this problem and thus must share the blame. The prevailing approach has been that it is the Indian who must adapt to the wage economy and the 40-hour week; any suggestion that the firms adapt their approach has been rejected, for the unsurprising reason that they could not risk innovations deleterious to their net revenues.

La Ronge, Saskatchewan, is the site of a small base metal mine which has in the past few years become an outstanding exception to this general rule. Considerable success has been met through special training programs and enlightened personnel policies that allow more adaptation to cultural differences.

The only federal government-owned mine in Canada is located at Uranium City, 300 miles north of La Ronge. In the heyday of uranium, this mine was one of several operating in the district; now slack markets and depressed prices are seriously affecting the profitability of the town's only real economic support. It has become a regional service centre of some importance and its three doctors serve a population estimated at 7000 persons, most of whom are residents of Indian settlements. Uranium City is served by air and, in the short summer season, by water transport that originates in Fort McMurray, Alberta. The company, which had its origins in the wartime takeover of strategic uranium deposits at Great Bear Lake, operates its own air service and provides free transportation to Edmonton at regular intervals for its employees and their families. The air service also transports the uranium concentrate in 600 pound barrels to railhead at Edmonton.

In the Northwest Territories, mining operations are carried on in four areas, and the scale of operations varies from that of the underground mine on Great Bear Lake, which produces 100 tons of high-grade silver–copper ore daily, to the open pit operations at Pine Point where the mill capacity is 8000 tons of lead–zinc ore per day. The Echo Bay mine, and to a lesser degree the mine at Tungsten north of Watson Lake and the gold mines at Yellowknife, are the archetype pioneering operations, where high costs occasioned by transportation charges, high inventory levels, and climatic factors are offset by the high unit value of the products; the ore at Echo Bay has a gross value of about $105 per ton. Conversely, exploitation of the Pine Point ore bodies awaited construction of a railroad, and efficient large scale open pit operations were necessitated by the ore grade which runs about $30 per ton.

While most of the population in the mining communities in the Northwest Territories depends for its livelihood on the fortunes of a single mine, Yellowknife presents an interesting contrast. To an increasing degree, Yellowknife is becoming less a gold mining town and more a government centre, as a result of its recent designation as territorial capital. The inevitable closure of the gold mines likely will not cause the disruptive effects that have been felt in other northern communities.

It has taken nearly 70 years for mineral production in the Yukon to rise to the levels experienced during the gold rush days. In the recent revival gold has played almost no part – less than 2 per cent of the Territory's production of $64 million in 1970 was made up of gold, much of it from small placer operations that still exist in the Dawson area. The major minerals in 1970 were copper, lead, zinc, and asbestos, added to the silver production which has come from the Keno Hill district for many years.

The largest mine in the Yukon is at Faro, where an open pit gives access to a lead–zinc ore body having a production life estimated at more than 30 years. From the mine, where a small townsite has been constructed, the concentrate goes by road to the railhead at Whitehorse, and thence to markets in Japan and West Germany.

Near Whitehorse, a large copper mine commenced operations in 1967 on deposits that had been worked in the early part of the century. A major advantage enjoyed by this firm was the proximity of a large town, which obviated the necessity to construct and maintain a townsite. At present the mine is shut down while development work is proceeding to enable resumption of operations.

Asbestos mining is new to the Yukon, but just south of its border with British Columbia, an open pit asbestos mine has been in production for 17 years. The high grade fibre is trucked 357 miles (575 km) to Whitehorse, from where it is shipped to world markets. The firm which operates this mine has vigorously searched for other asbestos deposits in the Cordillera, and in 1967 brought its mine at Clinton Creek near Dawson into production. Welcome as this new mine is, it is unfortunate that it is far enough from Dawson to prompt the construction of a new independent townsite. Dawson, where the last gold dredge ceased operations in late 1966, may capture some benefits from the new mine and its employees, but not enough to materially change its current position. The major linkage problem is the lack of a bridge over the Yukon River. During freeze-up and break-up, a tramway is the sole means of crossing the river; daily commuting is out of the question. Current estimates for a bridge are in the order of $6 million, and now that there are two separate townsites a bridge would have little effect on Dawson.

Benefits and Costs

It is clear then that, despite its problems, the industry has been of considerable benefit as an initiator and supporter of northern communities, and has contributed in a major way to national growth and prosperity. To complete the assessment, some consideration of the associated costs is necessary. We have already seen references to some direct financial costs. Here, then, we need only to consider briefly the social and environmental costs of northern mining as it has proceeded to date.

In any activity as dynamic as northern mining, social dislocation is inevitable. Each mine opening is a stimulus to immigration; each closure requires adaptation and mobility on the part of employees and their families, as well as others dependent on the income generated by the mine. In an isolated community, dominated by one employer, there is potential for a heavy-handed employer's attitude to prevail outside the work place, and this has occurred. The nature of the work combines with traditional employment attitudes to limit opportunities for women in the northern mineral industry; this has often resulted in communities with predominantly single male populations characterized by high turnover and social instability. A balanced appraisal must also take account of the many pleasant northern towns and villages based on mines: in Manitouwadge, Timmins, Flin Flon, one encounters the feeling that to live anywhere else is accepting second best.

If there is a uniquely northern social problem associated with mining, it is the failure to involve the indigenous people of the region in the economic activity. Too often they have been spectators only, or have been socially disrupted by the wave of development. To an increasing degree there will have to be explicit recognition of the need to subordinate traditional development objectives in the North to the well-being of the local inhabitants. Some steps in this regard have been taken in the past year notably north of 60°.

Environmental problems have been associated with mineral development since its beginnings, but it is of comparatively recent date that such effects were considered serious, except in a few instances. Even now, the increased concern over ecological costs is based largely in southern Canada, where a broader view of costs and benefits is said to prevail.

Mining has historically been assigned top rank in the hierarchy of resource uses in the north, as an examination of relevant provincial legislation would reveal. This has encouraged a division of lands into 'mineral lands' and 'waste lands,' in the minds of developers and administrators. As a result, companies have traditionally taken a narrow engineering approach to disposal of waste rock, tailings, and chemical reagents, as well as to the by-products of smelting and refining processes, where there was no commercial benefit from alternative procedures. The examples are numerous and well known: at Kirkland Lake, the community's namesake was filled with slimes from the gold mines; at Yellowknife, arsenic from gold refining temporarily contaminated the local water supply; at Sudbury, reagents released to local water courses create serious ecological problems, early smelting operations played havoc with surrounding vegetation; at Bathurst, finely ground tailings allow introduction of acidic compounds to a salmon stream; in the Yukon, exploration trenching by bulldozers has caused excessive erosion in several locations; at Elliot Lake, leakage from tailing dams allowed introduction of acidic compounds into the local watershed; a 'No Swimming' sign at the Trans-Canada highway picnic site downstream is one result.

There is evidence to suggest that new attitudes on the part of government and industry have come to prevail, so that the future environmental costs associated with mineral development will be kept to a minimum. The mining firms will still be faced with the problem of costs versus return: for example, a northern plant extracting sulphur from smelter stack gases is in competition with involuntary production of sulphur from natural gas wells, in an over-supplied market. Only government regulation will lead to extraction of stack gas sulphur in such as case. At the same time, it is necessary to take a balanced approach to environmental costs of mineral development in the North. In a balanced appraisal one must separate those problems of real ecological significance from instances which merely clash with our perception of what has aesthetic appeal.

Future Growth

Known deposits, as yet undeveloped, combine with favourable geological environments to assure continuing supplies of mineral resources in the North. If discussion is restricted to those areas north of 60°N, a manageable list can be assembled from east to west (Figure 4.6).

Two major deposits, one of nickel ore and another of asbestos, await exploitation in the Deception Bay area of Ungava. Enough development work has been performed to determine the technical feasibility of these projects but economic factors have thus far delayed commencement of production. In the same general region the existence of large iron deposits has been known for some time and periodically these receive attention. To date the most promising iron deposits in the eastern Arctic have been located in north-central Baffin Island. Active consideration was given to exploitation of this ore body, which grades better than 67 per cent iron, but a combination of market conditions and the physical problems inherent in production and shipping from such an area, where a short ice-free period would make stockpiling ('double mining') necessary, have delayed the project.

Another eastern Arctic mineral deposit is receiving attention again this year. At Arctic Bay on Baffin Island, lead–zinc bodies of considerable magnitude, and grades comparable to those being mined at Pine Point are being examined. This deposit is of particular interest and underground development work is currently underway.

Farther west, major but as yet uneconomic gold deposits are known to exist in the Contowoyto Lake District, and to the northwest, copper occurrences, some of them examined by Samuel Hearne in 1771, have received considerable attention, although to date reserves are not such as to warrant development. In the Cordillera of the Yukon, the past decade has witnessed discovery of several potentially major mineral bodies. Foremost among these are the Snake River iron deposits, the porphyry copper bodies northeast of Dawson, and lead–zinc prospects in the area around the new Anvil mine in central Yukon.

Figure 4.7 suggests the broad areas in which future discoveries and production of hardrock minerals could be expected. The point that must be stressed is that the map presents comparison *within* the Territories only; many geologists would consider other areas in Canada more attractive than the 'excellent' areas shown on the map, on the basis of rock formations and tectonic elements.

Notwithstanding the existence of these deposits and the potential for others, public attention has been monopolized by the search for oil and gas in the North, rather than on the more mundane hardrock developments. Exploration has been spurred by a combination of factors: rapidly increasing world demands for energy fuels, depletion of fields more adjacent to demand centres, favourable geological formations as shown in Figure 4.8, and, probably most important, by the recent discoveries at Prudhoe Bay in Alaska in 1968. The oil discoveries in the Mackenzie Delta, and the gas finds on King Christian and Melville Islands have accelerated the process. Through its 45 per cent participation in Panarctic Oils Limited, the major land holder in the Arctic Islands, the government of Canada has a major stake in the area's oil and gas resources; its financial contribution remains significant to the exploration effort.

Exploration expenditures for oil and gas in the North rose from $14.5 million in 1960 to $75.6 million in 1969. At the time of writing, several consortia were actively studying routes and techniques that would be suitable to bring gas or oil to markets, principally in the United States, while exploratory drilling was continuing in the Mackenzie Delta and the Arctic Islands. Geologists are generally encouraged by the prospects for commercial production, although a sizable body of opinion considers that exploitation may not come before 1980. An Arctic Island gas discovery, for example, requires extensive development drilling prior to a production

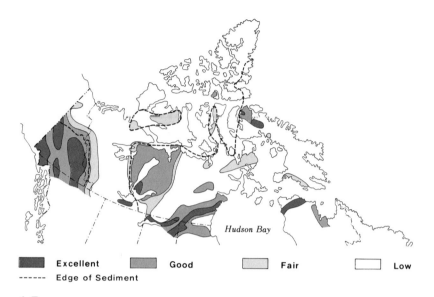

Excellent Good Fair Low
------ Edge of Sediment

4.7

Mineral Regions-Comparative Potential (except for Oil and Gas)

(Source: G. S. Barry, Recent Mineral Developments in Northern Canada (unpublished manuscript) 1969)

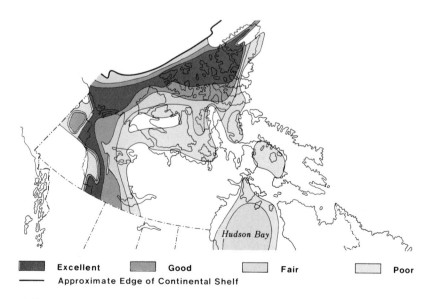

Excellent Good Fair Poor
—— Approximate Edge of Continental Shelf

4.8

Prospective Oil and Gas Regions

(Source: G. S. Barry, Recent Developments in Northern Canada (unpublished manuscript) 1969)

decision, and then the problem arises: how do we ship natural gas from King Christian Island, latitude 78°N, to markets in Canada or the United States? No pipelines have ever been built in such an unfavourable environment, across land and intervening seas, to reach the Arctic mainland, where problems are still sufficiently serious to present significant impediments. One of the most challenging tasks will be to cross ice-covered water, where the unconsolidated sea bed shows evidence of ice scouring that has left trenches up to 60 ft (18 m) deep. Figure 4.6 shows the tentative routes under consideration by various commercial groups.

It seems clear that development of the North's mineral resources will continue. Trends based on aggregate production values are extremely positive; within the broad picture the North will continue to witness mine openings, new petroleum developments, and, inevitably, exhaustion of individual deposits. Much of the region beyond the Boreal forest is still in the initial 'skimming' stage where high-unit values will be necessary to overcome the costs involved in frontier operations, although the improvements in mining and transport technology in this century have been so great that ore grades which 50 years ago would have been submarginal in southerly regions are now amenable to production in the North. However, the *relative* position of the North has not been much enhanced by such technological advances; outstanding projects are still required.

Predictions concerning mineral resource developments are notoriously difficult to make, but even more difficult is the assessment of the impact of these developments. What are the implications of these and other future mineral developments in the North? We have seen the impact of the mining industry and areas of mid-northern Canada; in this latter region we can expect to see continuation of the processes that have characterized the past 70 years: the filling of blanks as more sophisticated search techniques combine with improved mining and transport costs to bring into use additional deposits which have either remained undiscovered or are to date uneconomic. Conceivably a number of these additions will be made in areas close to existing mining camps, but some centres could in the next few decades drop from the list of viable mining towns. For many of these towns there is no alternative economic base that could maintain the community at anywhere near its present size: Uranium City, Red Lake, La Ronge, Val d'Or – each of these has developed other functions such as government and commercial services, or a growing tourist industry, but none of these functions shows any signs of offsetting the inevitable decline of the support resulting from mineral developments in the area.

To criticize the performance of the mining industry in instances of community decline is to forget that mines are impermanent fixtures in the regional landscape: if permanent settlement is expected, replacement support for the community is essential. All too often, this support has taken the form of subsidies designed to postpone the inevitable day of closure. There will be new mining towns, but how many? Much depends on policies evolving in the North with respect to regional centres; for example, how many centres per unit area of land are warranted? This presupposes resource information superior to that we now have, but intensive examination of the concept will promote a more rational approach, one that will reduce the problems encountered by temporary isolated communities.

The measure of success in northern mineral development is becoming less the dollar value of production, and more the real contribution to the region and its inhabitants. To provide for meaningful participation by the Indian and Eskimo in the process, a shift in priorities is required, and is slowly taking place. At the same time, there is by no means unanimity of opinion that participation in the industry is the optimum course for these northern people to follow; we have too seldom sought their view before we develop our plans for the North.

The environmental implications of future northern mineral development are of considerable importance, especially in connection with the exploitation and transmission of High Arctic oil or gas resources. The magnitude of the projects, the susceptibility of the area to long-term damage, and the pressure to develop the region's resources combine to instill urgency into studies of the north's ecology, and of means whereby it can be protected from unacceptable alteration. Similarly, there is an urgent need to assess the relative merits of designating areas of the North as reserves, wherein no economic activity will take place, or letting commercial and geological forces decide the allocation of land between competing uses. One of the problems here is that areas of unique scenic or environmental qualities are often that way because of geological factors that at the same time favour the existence of economic mineral deposits.

The combination of all these factors – the potential for increased production, the new areas to be opened up, the implications for economic, social and environmental issues – will make the next decade an interesting period in the northern parts of Canada.

5 The Population of Northern Canada

ROBERT M. BONE

The Canadian North is an enormous land mass with few people. With most Canadians huddled near the American border, our vast northern territory, stretching from the edge of Canada's ecumene to the islands of the Arctic Ocean, represents the most sparsely settled region of Canada. This emptiness reflects the peripheral geographical position of northern Canada. In the past, remoteness from markets and a weak infrastructure, as well as marginal agricultural resources, had inhibited settlement. In more recent decades, the booming mineral industry and the modernizing of native life have caused population increases and new patterns of settlement. Still, the most striking feature of the North is the sparsity of its population.

Canadian Development and the North
This polar region forms Canada's last undeveloped frontier. Since Confederation, the challenge of other frontiers has absorbed most of the nation's energy. The welding of colonies and territories into a nation was an awesome task, often running against the grain of geography and the forces of American continentalism. One result of this nation building has been to polarize our population along the American border, fittingly described in an American geography book (Trewartha, Robinson, and Hammond 1967, p. 542):

Canada's 20 million people appear to be drawn as by a magnet toward the giant-neighbor on the south, for they are strikingly concentrated along the United States border. The Canadian ecumene is a narrow belt some 2,800 miles long and only 100 to 200 miles wide. About 50 per cent of the settlement is within 100 miles of the Canadian–United States boundary, and 90 per cent is within 200 miles.

With the development of southern Canada now assured, the nation is taking a fresh look northwards. In recent years, national concern has been focussed upon arctic sovereignty, mineral development, and native peoples. A single project now under discussion, the Mackenzie Valley pipe-line route, could shape the settlement patterns for years to come. Whether the nation will attempt to direct development and settlement more than at present is unclear. What is clear is that the current developments are setting the framework for future population patterns.

While most Canadians foresee a modest expansion in northern develop-ment and settlement, a more optimistic view is held by Richard Rohmer, whose Mid-Canada Development concept calls for a national northern policy of planned development and settlement. His futuristic views (Roh-mer 1970, pp. 136–7) are as follows:

Let us suppose that Canada South continues to attract 95 per cent of Can-ada's total population. This would leave only five per cent to live in Mid-Canada and the Arctic.

To talk in terms of even five per cent means that we should prepare to ac-commodate in Mid-Canada a population of some six million by the year 2065, if we are to believe forecasts that our total population will increase by about 100 million within 100 years of our Centennial Year – 1967.

And, to bring things into closer focus, a total population of close to 40 mil-lion before the end of this century (which means that most of us will still be alive if not kicking) would provide two million people for the conservatively estimated five per cent due to live in Mid-Canada and the Arctic instead of in densely populated Canada South.

Certainly world conditions are more favourable for raw material de-velopment and export than ever before and this type of economic develop-ment, while subject to the shortcomings of foreign markets and price vacillations, appears destined for Canada's North. Such primary develop-ment, much of which is likely to be mineral extraction, will stimulate only a modest population growth. Constant emphasis upon highly automated mining operations coupled with continuing technological improvements in transportation suggests that a small highly skilled and well-paid labour force will migrate north and that resources, such as minerals, power, and timber, will be sent to existing industrial complexes in southern Canada, the United States, Japan, and western European countries. Furthermore, considering the existing remoteness from labour markets and the small and widely dispersed northern markets, significant private investments in the labour intensive secondary and tertiary sectors of the economy seems most unlikely. Even more unlikely is the channeling of large sums of pub-lic monies into such enterprises. For these reasons, some doubt may be cast upon the suggestion that by the end of this century the North's popu-lation will grow as rapidly as the country as a whole. Indeed, unless the economy shifts from such a heavy reliance upon capital intensive indus-tries to labour intensive ones, then the working force will remain small and highly skilled, and the native Canadians will conclude that such development of their lands is for the benefit of others.

By far the most critical human element in this development is the role of Canadians of Eskimo and Indian ancestry. With more and more northerners of this ethnic background opting for settlement life, their limited participation in the wage economy, while understandable in view of their poor competitive position in the labour market, is a serious flaw. Left uncorrected, the continued failure of these developments to involve such people could fester into serious social and political problems. Yet, with the course of northern development following along the lines of the staple theory, a regional economy is emerging which is dominated by primary industry whose production is almost entirely dependent upon foreign markets and which is characterized by a small but highly skilled labour force. Such development would be an empty thing for the Indians, Eskimos, and Métis, most of whom lack the experience and training for such employment. To this point, the Honourable Jean Chrétien (1969, p.1) revealed that in 1968 ...'these workers comprised only 5.3 per cent of the total mine labour force of the Northwest Territories, or 63 men out of a total of 1,182 workers. In the Yukon it was only 3.4 per cent of the total industry work force, or 28 men out of a total of 820.' Without a doubt, economic development of the North has by-passed the vast majority of the original inhabitants of this generation. The question is, what about the next generation?

Past Population Patterns
Prior to the Age of Discovery, the Indians and Eskimos practised a nomadic hunting life. Game, particularly caribou and seal, controlled their numbers and ordered their distribution. While Mooney (1928, p. 33) estimated that the aboriginal population of Canada prior to contact with Europeans was just over 220 thousand, with perhaps around one third of this population living in northern Canada, their way of life had little impact upon the land, making accurate estimates extremely difficult. Considering the limited command of the inhabitants over the environment, their numbers were likely small and, depending on the availability of game, subject to periods of expansion and contraction. Further, for most, the almost constant search for game necessitated a nomadic way of life. While certain locations were visited more frequently and, in some cases, these places became seasonal camp sites, permanent camps were rare.

A major feature of those days was the distribution of these hunting peoples into somewhat distinct geographical areas. The most striking aspect of this spatial pattern still exists, with the Eskimos located in the

Arctic and the Indians in the Subarctic. Within these two natural zones, groups of people occupied certain areas which constituted their hunting grounds. The Arctic contained the following Eskimo subcultural groups: Mackenzie, Copper, Netsilik, Iglulik, Caribou, South Baffin, and Labrador Eskimos. In the Subarctic, there were two major linguistic groups, the Athabascans and the Algonquins, and two minor groups, the Tlingit and the Tsimshian. The Athabascans, occupying most of the western section of the northern coniferous forest, consisted of the Beaver, Carrier, Chilcotin, Chipewyan, Dogrib, Hare, Kutchin, Loucheux, Nahani, Slave, and Yellowknife peoples, while the Algonquins, living mainly in the forested lands of Manitoba, Ontario, and Quebec were represented by the Algonkin, Cree, Montagnais, Naskapi, and Ojibway peoples (see Figure 5.1).

Following contact with the fur traders, migration occurred with bands of different linguistic affiliation occupying lands traditionally held by others. The search for beaver provided the rationale for these 'invasions' and the acquisition of the musket by Indians living in close proximity to the trading posts provided the necessary weaponry superiority to intimidate and sometimes to slaughter their unfortunate neighbours. A few Indian peoples, notably the Iroquois and the Cree, assumed the role of middlemen by securing furs from other Indians and then exchanging these furs at the trading posts where the terms of trade were most advantageous. Later, as trading posts spread across the country, the cordons of the middlemen were eventually breached. As well, with tribal hunting grounds frequently being challenged, tribal control of land was in a state of flux. According to Jenness (1955, pp. 254–5)

In eastern Canada, the Algonkians and Hurons, assisted by the French, assaulted their old enemies the Iroquois until the latter obtained firearms from the Dutch, vigorously assumed the offensive, and more than evened up the score. Micmac Indians crossing from Nova Scotia to Newfoundland completed the annihilation of the unfortunate Beothuk, and the Cree raided south and west over the Prairies, down the Mackenzie to its delta, and up the Peace River into the Rocky Mountains. In the north, the Chipewyans, obtaining guns at Churchill, oppressed the more distant Athapaskan tribes and kept them from visiting the trading post until smallpox decimated all the bands and the traders opened new posts on the Mackenzie.

During the fur trade era, the population of the North, while subject to considerable regional migrations, probably declined, perhaps by as much as half of Mooney's precontact population estimate of 220,000 (Jenness, pp. 1, 249–64; Mooney, p. 33). In 1881, the Indian population of Canada was estimated at just over 100,000 (Urquhart and Buckley 1965, p. 18). Starvation, disease, and warfare took their toll, while the cultural shock associated with the confrontation with European civilization be-

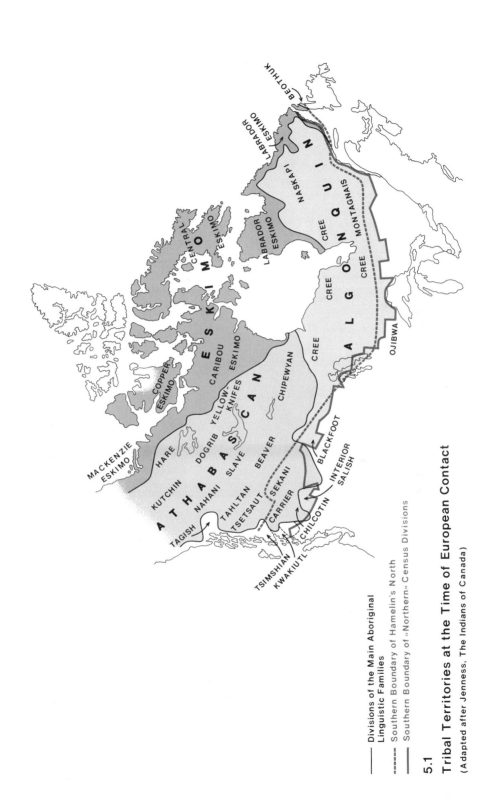

5.1

Tribal Territories at the Time of European Contact

(Adapted after Jenness, The Indians of Canada)

Divisions of the Main Aboriginal
Linguistic Families

------ Southern Boundary of «Hamelin's North

—— Southern Boundary of «Northern» Census Divisions

wildered the survivors. During this era, the North remained a sparsely populated land with a population well under 100,000 inhabitants, almost all of whom were Indians and Eskimos.

Fur posts were the only settlements. The trappers and hunters roamed across the barrens and through the forests for most of the year, coming to trade at the post maybe once or twice during that time. Only a handful of European traders and missionaries lived in the North. Yet these few people by offering trade and religion at these settlements bound the Indians to particular trading posts.

The Spread of Settlement Northwards

With the dawning of the mining era, Canadians of European descent began to migrate northwards. This migration increased the size of the North's population and in the process changed its distribution and ethnic composition. In the 1880s, the construction of the Canadian Pacific Railway through the Shield led to the discovery of a number of mineral deposits, some of which were on the edge of the boreal forest. Three decades later, the building of Canada's second transcontinental railway also led to mineral discoveries. However, the most famous mining development, the Klondike gold rush, lay many hundreds of miles north of these railways. Despite its isolation, thousands poured into the Yukon and Dawson City suddenly became one of the largest towns west of Winnipeg. By 1901, the Yukon had a population of just under 30,000, which may have represented close to a third of the North's people. However, with the collapse of the boom and the introduction of power dredges and other large-scale techniques of placer gold mining, people began to drift away from the gold fields. By 1921, the precarious nature of settlements based upon a mining economy was abundantly clear, for the Yukon's population had dropped to just over 4000.

Since these early years, the North has witnessed many new mining ventures, some of which have provided a much sounder basis for settlement. Schefferville, Thompson, Pine Point, and Faro are examples of towns based upon the exploitation of large mineral deposits. Consequently, their life span is expected to be much longer than that of the Klondike. These urbanite newcomers to the Subarctic are often described as southern transplants, whose willingness to remain in the North is frequently overtaxed by environment. Understandably, a high rate of labour turnover has troubled these communities.

Then, too, the surge of military activity in the early 1940s and again in the 1950s brought thousands of troops and construction workers into the North. However, once the urgent construction was completed and the

Table 5.1   Population of Northern Canada, 1931–61
(*Census of Canada* 1931–66)

	1931	1941*	1951	1961	1966
Population	402,077	537,057	686,530	1,029,448	1,171,374
% of Canada	3.8	4.6	4.9	5.6	5.8
Indian–Eskimo	50,985	56,454	71,764	97,291	N/A
% of North	12.7	10.5	10.5	9.5	N/A

*Includes 1945 figures for Census Subdivision 10 of Newfoundland.

military threat diminished, these workers and service personnel quickly departed. It is clear that the white worker has rarely taken root in the Arctic and his adaptability to the Subarctic has been less than spectacular, partly because both private and public enterprises liberally transfer their staff from region to region and partly because the North's economy lacks stability. Still, regardless of these comings and goings, over the long haul there has been a net gain of population from migration, and today the Euro-Canadian elements of the North dominate especially in developed areas of the Subarctic.

Recent Changes and the Position of Native and Foreign Workers
The population of the North is increasing. At the turn of the century, there may have been around 100,000 people. By 1931, it was just over 400,000. Today there is close to one and a quarter million people in the North. This growth is associated with the influx of migrants from the south and, in recent decades, with a high rate of natural increase among northerners. The migration to the North has been triggered by economic development, especially in the field of mining. The population of new mining towns has originated in southern Canada where the main pool of skilled labour is located. The North, by offering attractive jobs, has drawn heavily from this pool. As well, the federal government's policy to expand its operations in the two territories has greatly increased the number of civil servants living north of 60° (Table 5.1).

Since the 1950s, the native peoples have greatly increased their numbers, owing to a rise in their rate of natural increase. In 1951 there were 71,764 Indians and Eskimos, while a decade later their numbers had increased to 97,291. To a considerable degree, this increase reflects the decline in the death rate which can be attributed to the extension in the 1950s of public health and welfare programs into northern communities. In addition, the educational and low rental housing programs have stimulated the process of urbanization. Now almost all the people live in settle-

Table 5.2   Immigrant population, by period of immigration and by territories (*Canada Yearbook 1966*, p. 224)

Territory	Before 1930	1931–40	1941–5	1946–50	1951–5	1955–61
Yukon	867	81	42	265	833	1724
Northwest	425	114	37	178	737	1387
Total	1292	195	79	443	1570	3111

ments. Conversely, the accumulated effect of urban life has turned the younger generation away from the traditional life of hunting and trapping. Yet, with only a handful holding permanent jobs, most subsist on rations and other forms of welfare. Also, since few jobs are available in these isolated settlements, labour mobility is a necessary fact of life, but is largely inoperable because of the cultural gap between 'native' settlements and 'white' towns. One of the consequences of this situation is that almost half of Canada's native population receives welfare assistance, compared with 3.5 per cent of the general public (Indian-Eskimo Association of Canada).

Within the North, a considerable proportion of the migrant population is foreign born. The two territories provide some insight into the importance of non-Canadian born migrants. In 1961, the foreign-born population of the Yukon Territory was 2714 and for the Northwest Territories, it was 1963 (*Canada Yearbook 1966*, p. 224). In both cases when native Indians and Eskimos are excluded the percentage of foreign-born in the territories in 1961 was slightly over 20 per cent (21.9 per cent for the Yukon Territory and 20.1 per cent for the Northwest Territories), which is somewhat above the national average of 15.6 per cent. The implication of the figures in Table 5.2 suggests that there may be some truth in the popular notion that white Canadian-born people are more reluctant to live in the North than foreign-born Canadians. Certainly both private and public enterprises have made special efforts to recruit foreigners, claiming that Canadians will not go North.

The Paradox of High and Low Mobility

Generally, the geographical and job mobility is high for the southern migrant and low for the locally born northerners. Two of the principal problems facing industry and government are the high degree of job turnover, which raises recruitment and training costs and prevents the establishment of an experienced labour force, and the limited job qualifications of most

Table 5.3   Territorial migrants five years of age and over, 1956–61
(*Canada Yearbook 1966*, p. 187)

Province	Origin of immigrants to the territories	Destination of emigrants from the territories	Net change of territorial population
Newfoundland	55	50	5
Prince Edward Island	52	62	− 10
Nova Scotia	152	160	− 8
New Brunswick	140	98	42
Quebec	384	413	− 29
Ontario	1159	1529	−370
Manitoba	429	379	50
Saskatchewan	570	516	54
Alberta	1862	1807	59
British Columbia	1411	1882	−471
Total	6214	6896	−682

native northerners. Paradoxically, in the 1960s, the North was plagued with both shortages of labour and underemployment of labour. With no solution in sight, welfare expenditures and northern allowances inevitably will become larger and larger.

The interprovincial origin of the territorial population and the mobility of the territorial population throw some light on the character of the North's population. To what degree the current situation in the territories is indicated by the figures for 1965–71 and to what degree they are comparable to that of the North as a whole is unknown. However, while these figures for the territories may indicate the extreme conditions, there are signs that somewhat similar conditions hold true for the northern portions of the provinces.

These figures also indicate the degree of mobility. For example, in the territories the total departures and arrivals during 1956–61 (Table 5.3) totalled 13,110 or over half of those who reported their usual place of residence in 1956. However, compared with the fact that approximately 10 per cent of the national population was involved in this interprovincial and territorial migration, the difference is significant and suggests a lack of stability in the territorial population originating in the provinces.

The North: A Question of Definition
In this chapter, the North is referred to as comprising the Arctic and Subarctic zones of Canada. Yet to examine the population of the North,

Table 5.4   Population of Northern Canada by census subdivisions, 1961 and 1966 (*Census of Canada 1961* and *1966*)

| Census subdivision | 1961 | | | 1966 |
	Total	Indian Eskimo	Native (%)	Total
Yukon Territory	14,628	2,207	15.1	14,382
Franklin District, N.W.T.	5,758	4,432	77.0	7,167
Keewatin District, N.W.T.	2,345	1,948	83.1	2,886
Mackenzie District, N.W.T.	14,895	6,853	46.0	18,685
B.C. 9	38,203	6,968	18.2	48,265
8	74,240	7,000	9.4	103,767
10	31,061	1,161	3.7	41,404
Alberta 15	76,884	7,959	10.4	88,344
12	47,310	5,547	11.7	50,635
Saskatchewan 18	20,708	9,813	47.4	21,126
Manitoba 16	46,781	15,332	32.8	54,389
Ontario 20 (Kenora)	51,474	10,217	19.8	53,995
47 (Thunder Bay)	138,518	3,890	2.8	143,673
5 (Cochrane)	95,666	2,224	2.3	97,334
Quebec A (Abitibi)	11,321	484	4.3	17,896
B (Mistassini)	1,796	1,718	95.7	1,938
C (Nouveau-Quebec)	8,121	4,377	53.9	8,986
34 (Lac St Jean)	105,230	1,045	1.0	105,909
16 (Chicoutimi)	157,196	76	0.0	161,773
60 (Saguenay)	81,900	7,192	8.8	107,663
Nfld. 10 (Labrador)	13,534	1,225	9.1	21,157
Total	1,029,448	97,291	9.5	1,171,374

census units offer the only statistical units. Unfortunately, the southern limit of the Subarctic and certain census subdivisions are not in perfect harmony. The major shortcomings involve the incorporation of parts of the relatively densely populated farming areas of the Peace River district and the Lac St Jean area into otherwise non-farming lands of the Subarctic. In Ontario, the boreal forest extends both north and south of certain northern designated census subdivisions. In the Cordillera, the zonal pattern of natural vegetation is interrupted by its high elevations and rugged topography, making the identification of the Subarctic's southern limit almost impossible.

Nevertheless, the census subdivisions identified in Table 5.4 provide the best possible fit with the Arctic and Subarctic zones and offer a useful statistical vehicle for describing and analysing the population in the northern half of seven provinces and the two territories (Figure 5.2).

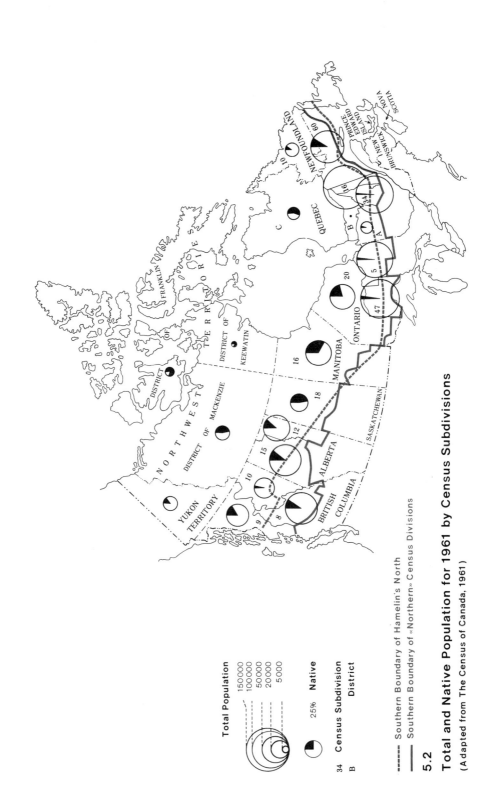

Total Population

150000
100000
50000
20000
5000

25% ▨ Native

34 Census Subdivision

B District

- - - - Southern Boundary of Hamelin's North
——— Southern Boundary of «Northern» Census Divisions

5.2

Total and Native Population for 1961 by Census Subdivisions

(Adapted from The Census of Canada, 1961)

Regional Patterns

An axiom of the geography of world population is its uneven distribution. This axiom is also valid for the Canadian North where most of the people are in a few small pockets and where most of the land is virtually uninhabited. For example, in 1966, the range of densities of population by census subdivision extended from 0.02 persons per square mile in the Northwest Territories to 162 in Chicoutimi (*Census of Canada, 1966*).

The distribution of population by provinces and territories also emphasizes an uneven pattern. Nearly two-thirds of the North's population is in Quebec and Ontario and almost one-third in the four western provinces. The territories and Newfoundland contain less than 5 per cent of this population. Further evidence of the highly concentrated nature of the North's population is revealed in the fact that over two-thirds of the people are found in seven census subdivisions (Chicoutimi, Saguenay and Lac St Jean of Quebec, Thunder Bay and Cochrane of Ontario, subdivision 8 of British Columbia, and subdivision 15 of Alberta).

Such a pattern of settlement strongly reflects the regional variation in northern development. It has drawn most Canadians into a few areas of the Subarctic and has urbanized Canadians of Indian and Eskimo ancestry, resulting in a highly concentrated population, with vast empty reaches.

Within the two major natural regions, the Arctic and the Subarctic, this unevenness reaches extreme proportions. The Arctic, with a population of some 20,000, has an exceptionally low density of population. While most are living in settlements, few centres contain over 1000 people. Ethnically, this region where approximately three-quarters of the people speak Eskimo is the last large territory with a non-white majority.

The region's commercial base is limited, with trapping still very important both in terms of total earned income and in terms of employment. While there is considerable exploratory activity, only a few mines were ever developed and these mines all had a short existence. As a result of the limited commercial activity, few whites have been attracted to this region, with the exception of administrators, teachers, nurses, police, missionaries, and a few others. Most of these people are employees of the federal government and have been sent North. Because the job mobility of most Eskimo-speaking peoples is limited, very few leave the Arctic for employment. At the same time, the absence of commercial activities has kept the numbers of whites low and those that venture into the Arctic rarely remain for more than ten years.

The Subarctic contains about 98 per cent of the North's people, most of whom live near its southern margins. While a significant minority are of Indian descent, over 90 per cent are of European background. The region's commercial base is much broader than that of the Arctic. Primary industries, such as mining and forestry, account for the bulk of production. In recent years, the mining industry has created new towns and has attracted people into the North. Cassiar in British Columbia, Faro in the Yukon, Pine Point in the Northwest Territories, Uranium City in Saskatchewan, Thompson in Manitoba, Schefferville in Quebec, and Labrador City in Newfoundland are examples of mining towns founded in the 1950s and 1960s. Although these towns are associated with huge mineral reserves, their dependency on a single resource binds them to the vicissitudes of world markets. Then too, regardless of the size of the resources, the non-renewable nature of mineral deposits places such settlements in an unfavorable position. With so much of the Subarctic's population based on mining, the long-term implications for these towns and villages are abundantly clear. Without diversification, much of which can only be achieved through greater processing and manufacturing of the mineral resources, the economic base of the North will remain narrow and vulnerable. Consequently, a large permanent population in the North seems unlikely.

Ethnic Patterns
The North contains nearly half of Canada's Indians and virtually all of her Eskimos. These radically distinct Canadians form just under 10 per cent of the northern population as against one per cent of the nation's population. As a consequence, they constitute a more important minority in the North than in Canada. With their natural rate of increase about triple that of the Canadian average and with approximately half of them under the age of 16, their importance as a group is not diminishing. The challenge facing these Canadians and Canadian society is their successful transfer from a primitive quasi-subsistence economy to a modern commercial one. As Father Andre-Pierre Steinmann (1970, p. 19) notes, 'C'est un gros problème. On n'a pas assez de positions, pas assez d'emplois, dans le Nord, pour placer tous ces jeunes-là.'

While the roots of this change began with the first days of European involvement in the North, recent events have generated new forces calling for rapid social change. With the rate of change in the 1970s expected to accelerate, the question is whether employment opportunities will keep pace. If not, the social fabric of northerners will be severely tested.

In general, the geographical distribution of these Canadians has three notable aspects. First, almost all now live in settlements: most of them in tiny settlements with a high proportion of natives (over 75 per cent);

those in larger centres usually live in the native area. This urbanization of native Canadians began in earnest some twenty years ago; before that time, few lived in communities. Changes in government policies did much to trigger this process, especially the programs advocating schools in northern communities and subsidized housing for northerners.

Secondly, the ethnic character of the North is influenced by the degree of commercial development: the weaker the commercial base, the higher the proportion of native Canadians. For example, in 1961 at Black Lake in Saskatchewan (95 per cent Chipewyan) and in Health District E4 of the Northwest Territories, which includes Boothia Peninsula, Somerset Island, Prince of Wales Island, and King William Island (95 per cent Eskimo), few commercial enterprises could be found and, consequently, few southern Canadians were present. Where commercial activities and public administration have occurred, involvement of local people has been slight, sometimes because they have not had the desire for most types of private and public employment, but more often because they lacked the qualifications. Some employers' stereotyped perception of natives as lazy and unreliable is also an employment barrier. Consequently, the developed areas and communities tend to be associated with white Canadians and underdeveloped areas and communities with native Canadians. The percentage of Indian and Eskimo peoples by census subdivisions (Table 5.4), tends to vary in accordance with the degree of economic development. Such a geographical relationship provides certain advantages to the minority, with isolation acting as a protective cultural shield. Balanced against this unique social milieu are the disadvantages associated with life in an underdeveloped area.

Thirdly, the geographical and occupational mobility of the native Canadians is low. The main hindrances to increased mobility are a deep cultural attachment to the local milieu and a limited ability to compete in the local and national job market. As a result, during the early 1960s, the per capita earnings from gainful employment of native Canadians were reported as less than one-quarter that of other northern Canadians (Hawthorn 1966, I, pp. 45, 85). With an increasing number of young people growing accustomed to urban life and employment, labour mobility may rise with more young people moving to towns and cities in search of work. While the concept of public subsidization of local industries is not unknown in Canada South, small native settlements and reserves of the North have yet to taste many of these fruits of Canadian life. In the 1970s, without a substantial increase in public supported developments in local areas, mobility will likely increase among the better educated young people, leaving the rest stranded in an economically depressed world where welfare dominates local life.

Urban Geography

Except for a handful of farmers, trappers, and hunters, northerners are almost entirely aggregated into settlements. Granted, the majority of these urban centres are tiny villages with populations of less than 1000 which, according to the Dominion Bureau of Statistics, are classified as rural. In the Northwest Territories, such a definition of urban centres meant that in 1966, although virtually all lived in settlements, only some 40 per cent of the population fell into the classification of urban dwellers. Irrespective of this definition, towns and villages house almost all northerners (Wonders 1960).

Only a few urban centres of the North are of medium size and none really qualify as region growth centres. In 1966, twelve towns had populations over 10,000 and five over 20,000 (Figure 5.3). The largest city was Port Arthur with a population in 1966 of 48,340, closely followed by its nearby neighbour, Fort William, with 48,208. In that year the population of towns with over 10,000 inhabitants comprised approximately 25 per cent of the total population of the North, compared with a national figure of approximately 50 per cent. The explanation for this difference probably lies in the particular development of the North. For example, the large number of small settlements reflects the many 'native' communities, which often have little commercial base and whose citizens' principal source of income is 'unearned,' and the single resource communities, whose economic base is designed to support a small but highly paid working force.

Urban centres of the North are often characterized by an atmosphere of isolation which fosters a distinct northern identity. The feeling of isolation stems from the limited and costly transportation and communciation links with southern Canada. While economic self-sufficiency may be promoted by high freight costs, the dependence on the outside world for a wide variety of goods and services is common to northern towns. The distinct social identity may be due to the openness of small communities and to the limited external social contact, such as television, movies, and live entertainment, forcing local substitutes. Finally, the fact that many towns are dominated by a single industry often provides such northern communities with a company town atmosphere.

For many of the smaller centres, there is no meaningful economic base and little wage employment. These villages are in reality collection basins

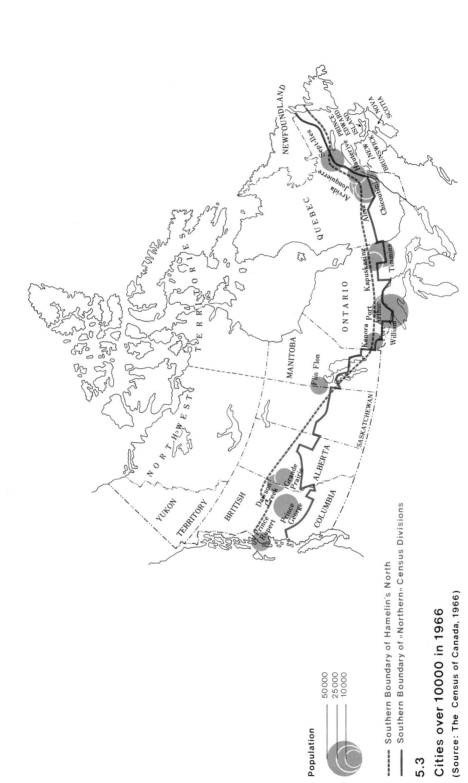

Population

50 000
25 000
10 000

- - - - - Southern Boundary of Hamelin's North
———— Southern Boundary of «Northern» Census Divisions

5.3

Cities over 10000 in 1966

(Source: The Census of Canada, 1966)

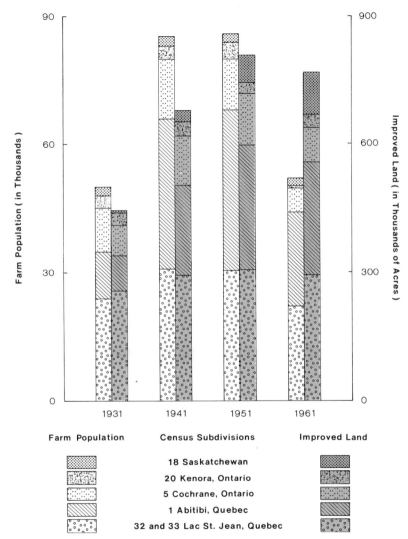

Note: Scale of diagram does not permit figures for Yukon and N.W.T. to be shown.

5.4

Agricultural Change in Northern Areas, 1931-1961

for recently 'urbanized' hunting and trapping peoples. Villages, e.g. Black Lake in Saskatchewan, provide a central place for the establishment of government services, such as education, health, job training, and subsidized housing. The availability of such public services plus generous welfare supports has spelled an end to the extended family hunting camps and isolated trappers' cabins.

The dominance of the urban population is a sign of the realities of the northern environment. Unlike Canada South, rural population based upon agriculture is of little consequence and appears to be declining, especially in Ontario and Quebec. The family farm is unknown in the Arctic and is rare in the Subarctic except for a few pockets in the Canadian Shield of Ontario and Quebec, notably the Clay Belt and Lac St Jean.

Over the last thirty years, these farm units have been under pressure and, in most regions, there has been a substantial retreat from the land. Figure 5.4 indicates that the most marked change took place in Ontario and Quebec. In both of the provinces, pioneers settled these lands in the past, when farming life was relatively more attractive, both socially and economically.

While, no doubt, northern agricultural production can be substantially increased, economically such an expansion cannot be justified at the present time. The problem of northern agriculture is partly one of marginal quality of land and limitations of climate and partly one of small-scale operations with high per unit production costs and limited markets. In addition, the ability of food produced outside the North to penetrate effectively and capture most of the northern market is a principal factor in limiting northern farming. Referring to the territories, (Rea 1968, p. 175) stated that 'it appears unlikely, therefore, that much more than one-tenth of one per cent of the food requirements in the Yukon and Northwest Territories in 1961 would have been produced locally.'

Even though the North's population is almost entirely found in settlements or towns, not one of these is large enough to function as a regional capital. Such cities are found only in Canada South. Owing to the regional character of Canada, there is a distinct areal division of Canada's North into city hinterlands. In broad terms, Montreal dominates the eastern sector, including Quebec and the eastern Arctic, while Toronto commands the trading area of Ontario and the central Arctic. St John's, Quebec City, Ottawa, and Thunder Bay function at a lower urban level in restricted areas of the Montreal and Toronto spheres of trade dominance. Vancouver and Edmonton share the western sectors of the North, although Saskatoon's share of influence extends over much of northern Saskatchewan, and Winnipeg's over northern Manitoba and the District of Keewatin.

To some degree, the regional nature of Canada's North is recorded in the major air transportation companies serving this part of Canada. The map of major regional airlines, consisting of Eastern Provincial, Quebecair, Nordair, Transair, Norcanair, Pacific Western, and Canadian Pacific airlines stresses the north–south transportation linkages which tie the regional capitals to their northern hinterlands.

The major urban centres of Canada's North are clustered along its southern margin and are linked to Canada's ecumene by road, rail, and air. To some degree, these towns are expressions of the regional character of the North's geography and political structure. Geography dictates the broad limits of northern regions while provincial and territorial governments strain to provide economic stimuli for urban centres within their respective political units. In 1966, the six largest cities, with populations exceeding 20,000, were all situated in the southern portion of the Subarctic, north of 60°; the largest town was Whitehorse with a population of just under 5000.

By geographic accident, Thunder Bay, an amalgamation of Port Arthur and Fort William, is classified as a northern city because it lies within the boreal forest. Yet this city, at a lower latitude than Vancouver, is part of the narrow developed corridor of Canada South through which the national transportation system flows (Canadian National and Canadian Pacific railways, Air Canada and Canadian Pacific, and the Trans Canada Highway). It is also the western terminal of the St Lawrence Seaway. While on the basis of natural vegetation, Thunder Bay is in the North, the national transportation system firmly incorporates this city into southern Canada.

Although there are common features to northern urban centres, Thompson, Manitoba, and Black Lake, Saskatchewan, represent distinctly different settlements. The former owes its existence to mining, while the latter is more an expression of social change than of economic development.

The city of Thompson, founded in 1957 by the International Nickel Company of Canada, is near a huge nickel deposit in an area of discontinuous permafrost. Only fifteen years ago, this townsite was a wilderness of coniferous forests and wildlife, inhabited by Indian trappers, and located some 400 miles (644 km) north of Winnipeg in the lake-covered Canadian Shield. Today, it is a mining community that represents a modern version of the frontier town and is connected to the south by the Canadian National Railway, gravel-surface highway 391, and Transair.

Thompson, with its neatly designed circular street pattern, modern bungalows, and shopping centres, is a replica of suburbia. Only the phys-

5.5

Distribution of Population, 1961

(Adapted from The Atlas of Canada)

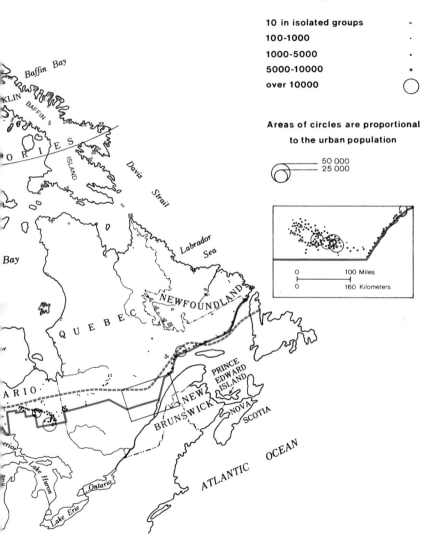

Population

10 in isolated groups	∘
100-1000	·
1000-5000	·
5000-10000	•
over 10000	◯

**Areas of circles are proportional
to the urban population**

50 000
25 000

0   100 Miles
0   160 Kilometers

- - - - - - -   Southern Boundary of Hamelin's North

━━━━━━   Southern Boundary of «Northern» Census Division

ical presence of the towering headframes and smokestacks of the refinery some two miles from the centre of town distinguishes Thompson from a modern suburb of Winnipeg. However, the social and economic life of the city is bound to the Inco operation and a company town atmosphere exists.

Like most mining settlements of the North, its population has been almost entirely drawn from the outside. Over the last 15 years, this immigration has created the largest town in northern Manitoba. In 1961, the population of Thompson was 3418 (Census of Canada 1961) and by 1966, it had nearly tripled to 8848 (Census of Canada 1966). In 1967, Thompson was incorporated as a city and its estimated size in 1971 was 23,000.

Black Lake, a Chipewyan settlement of about 500 people, is located in northern Saskatchewan some 500 miles north of Saskatoon. Unlike Thompson, Black Lake is an isolated village with limited transportation services. The main transportation link with the south is provided by Norcanair, which offers daily summer flights and three winter flights per week to Stony Rapids, a small community of Métis and whites some 14 miles (23 km) north of Black Lake. The Northern Transportation Company, which has two scheduled sailings (barges) to Stony Rapids in June and August, transports most of the supplies for the Hudson's Bay store, the prefabricated houses, oil, and other bulky goods.

The community of Black Lake is the home of the Stony Rapids band of Chipewyan Indians. While the Black Lake area was a frequently visited hunting and camping area before World War II, in 1952 a permanent settlement was established. By 1956, the population was 171 (Census of Canada 1956). Today it is approximately 500. This increase can be attributed to the high rate of natural increase, perhaps 3 per cent per year, and the movement of people from the nearby site of Stony Lake to Black Lake. The main attractions of Black Lake are the provincial school, Hudson's Bay store, the Roman Catholic church and the availability of subsidized housing, welfare, and wage employment. While there is a nursing station at Black Lake, the two nurses (one federally and the other provincially employed) live at the Stony Rapids' nursing station.

The economic base of Black Lake is virtually non-existent. Less than ten families still spend a substantial part of the year in the bush hunting and trapping and, with only two permanent jobs in the community held by Chipewyans (Hudson's Bay clerk and a teaching aid), welfare and occasional wage employment provides the bulk of the income for the inhabitants of the settlement. As most school-aged children appear attracted to settlement life and wage employment, hunting and trapping seem to be disappearing as a way of life.

Conclusion

During the twentieth century, the North's population has increased as commercial developments have drawn migrants northwards. Moreover, a high rate of natural increase of native Canadians over the last several decades has supplemented this population increase. In the next decade, the pace of population growth will be affected by important economic and social development. Imagine the impact of a Mackenzie transportation corridor. The rate of development in the western sector of the North would be greatly accelerated, the population pattern shaped for decades to come, and the social milieu transformed. Like the transcontinental railway, a Mackenzie corridor of pipelines, roads and a railway is an expression of national destiny and demands national control.

The North will continue to be a land of towns and villages unevenly spread across the forest and tundra. A few regional centres may grow and many smaller ones may stagnate or die. Mining towns will continue to come and go, although a few, such as Yellowknife, may be fortunate enough to develop other functions. Native settlements characterized by weak commercial foundations will probably be abandoned sometime in the future, presumably when the population has acquired sufficient social and labour mobility to move to centres with employment opportunities. Migration that destroys social structure and community pride solves nothing and only transfers poverty from one geographical area to another. We need no more disasters like Dene Village at Churchill.

The North is a paradox – company presidents complain about the cost of labour, its high turnover and scarcity, and the Minister of Northern Development and Indian Affairs worries about the ever-growing welfare payments and the lack of participation of native Canadians in northern development. Employers the world over recognize that an inexperienced worker with little or no schooling is often less productive than an experienced worker with schooling. In the North, many native Canadians are not fully accustomed to the western industrial society which causes employers to be leary. For these reasons alone, it is understandable why so few native Canadians have been involved in northern development. Perhaps such realities should be recognized and, once initial productivity differences have been established, employers of such labour should receive a subsidy to offset the lower productivity. Presumably, this subsidy would not strain the public purse since such a program should reduce welfare

Population

10	○
50	·
500	•
1000	●

5.6

Distribution of Indian and Eskimo Population, 1961

(Adapted from The Atlas of Canada)

payments. Furthermore, such programs should be regarded as a job train-ing scheme designed to have long-term social and economic returns, such as having children grow up in a working rather than a welfare atmos-phere. A subsidized economy of this kind would cover the transitional period from a hunting life to an industrial one. The hope is that, given several years of such a program, productivity would rise and employers' fears would be removed. When that point had been reached, native Cana-dians could compete on a more equal footing with other Canadians. Along the same lines, some attention should be given to replacing welfare pay-ments with subsidized activities in small native settlements until mobility is improved. These activities could include the establishment of forest operation in the upper Mackenzie to supply the raw materials for a pre-fabricated housing plant at a larger centre such as Yellowknife, snow-mobile repair and supply depots at several key centres, as well as price support of the traditional hunting and trapping economy.

Over the short run, the northern problem of full participation in Cana-dian society by native Canadians can be alleviated but not solved. Forces have been turned loose which have destroyed the old ways and have not yet created new ones. This is the case across the Polar World. The jump from a primitive life to an industrial life is fraught with hazards. Eco-nomic, social, demographic, and geographic changes of this magnitude de-mand a national purpose and justify a national strategy.

6 Politics of Canada's North

J. K. STAGER

It is a simple act to open a good atlas or select loose maps to see the place and shape of lands and seas in northern Canada. It is equally simple to look at maps on a world scale so that relative size and location of the Canadian North may be compared with other regions. But there are many ways of comprehending these locational and distributional facts, and where matters of government are concerned, a variety of backgrounds and motives channel political acts of discourse and decision. No matter what the scale – be it the international one where nation-states promote self-interested views of northern Canada, or the national where varying levels of government within Canada seek special consideration for their particular solution to northern political problems – the ingredients of politics are much the same. Since the period of discovery and exploration the factors entering political debate about the North have very much altered, mainly because of changes in the technology of transportation and communications. In addition, technology has turned physical and biological elements of the northern landscape into resources which, because they have value to man, need to be governed in some way. It is an interesting task to chronicle the political development in the Canadian North from the earliest days to the present, although this chapter is not designed for that purpose. Suffice it to note that, in contrast with past ignorance and lack of interest, renewed concerns about the northland of Canada have led to wider knowledge of, and attention to, the political geography of this region. Canadians were never more sensitive than they are today to the great range of factors which involve their north country, and about which political decisions need to be taken.

The politics of Canada's North may be considered from two initial viewpoints: these may be termed *external* and *internal*. The external viewpoint is the international one, where nations other than Canada evolve and adopt a comprehension or attitude to the Canadian North consistent with their own national goals or international commitments. The internal viewpoint is a wholly Canadian one; it is how Canadians comprehend and regard the northern part of their own country. The external and internal views draw upon common evidence but do not always coincide. External political action based upon external perception will provoke internal responses determined by internal concepts and plans. The opposite is also true. This chapter will consider first the external view, and later the internal view.

The Political Geography of the Canadian North: the External View

The environmental image that most foreigners[1] have of the Canadian north is an imperfect version of the true Arctic. It is taken to be a land of ice, snow, low temperatures and, for much of the year, darkness. It is inhabited by Eskimos who are renowned around the world as hardy people with lives that are exquisitely adjusted to a harsh land. To this caricature we can add the heroic image of the Royal Canadian Mounted Police guarding the national frontiers. It would be a grave error to suggest that the popular image is shared by foreign governments or business concerns who have an interest in the north polar region; they are not ill-informed about the Canadian North. Countries like those of Scandinavia or the USSR have within their territories a similar environmental gradient extending towards the pole. The state of Alaska provides a natural northern experience for the United States of America. Moreover, Canada has been generous to other nations in sharing knowledge of her northland, and many non-Canadian expeditions have been welcomed to the pursuit of northern science in Canadian national territory. Just as there is understanding of the different northern environments in Canada, there is common agreement about what northern lands are Canadian territory. At present no nation disputes that the islands bounded by the northern mainland of North America between 60° and 141° west longitude extending to the north pole are Canadian. The northern margin of Canada's north is, therefore, relatively easily defined; the southern margin has *not* been agreeably defined, even within Canada.

The importance of Canada's North, as perceived by foreign nations, is conditioned by their own national motives or goals. Such objectives may be directed to bilateral relations with Canada, or with other nations where Canadian northern territory plays a conditioning role. For example, Canada co-operated with the United States in building the Alaska Highway which fulfilled a national objective of the USA to have a land link to its northern territory, and at the same time was a mutual advantage for

---

1 It is difficult to write about the politics of northern Canada from a platform in space. As a Canadian, I chose a locus within Canada and use the terminology of Canadians.

Canada and the United States in its anxiety about continental defence during World War II. Currently, it is hard to believe that the USSR and the USA contemplate each other without being aware of northern Canada which lies between. These examples relate to the fundamental consideration of relative location. The whole of the north polar region for centuries was remote, inaccessible, and regarded as worthless. The empty land and frozen seas formed a barrier to surface travel and exchange. Before air travel, this barrier distorted the world's northern hemispheric connections from the closest and least expensive great circle routeways to longer journeys via the warmer oceans and settled land corridors. International air transport has changed this, and zones of dense human occupance may now be reached by shortest distance courses across the empty north. Routes from western Europe to western North America overfly directly and centrally the Canadian Arctic. Links to Japan from Europe are 'trans-polar,' as are routes between Japan and eastern North America. Overflying a national territory has led to the concept of national air space, and nations regulate the users of their national air space. Commercial flying around the world follows air space control sanctified by international agreements to which Canada subscribes. In addition to permitting foreign air carriers to cross the Canadian north, Canada provides navigational and weather forecasting assistance to overflights. It also is prepared for search and rescue operations should they ever be required. Such outward generosity – the wide Canadian 'sector' of Arctic territory means a small nation assumes longer flight-support responsibility – is traded in stern negotiation on behalf of Canadian air carriers operating into other countries.

The international co-operation of commercial aviation is in stark contrast to the independent and inflexible positions taken by national governments in a variety of other international arenas. Since World War II the earth's nations have not been allowed to sink back into the comfort of international peace and goodwill that the end of that war was supposed to bring. Mistrust between countries or allied groups of nations has been present, and, although not the only example to cite, the United States of America and the Union of Soviet Socialist Republics have many outstanding differences. That these two nations have opposed one another in varying degrees of intensity on the world political scene has placed Canada, and its northland, in an obviously strategic position (Figure 6.1). At times in the past when a divided world feared military adventure and countermove, the polar region was the avenue of engagement. The military technology of twenty years ago dictated that Canadian territorial space, particularly the northern zone, would be the first line of contact/defence

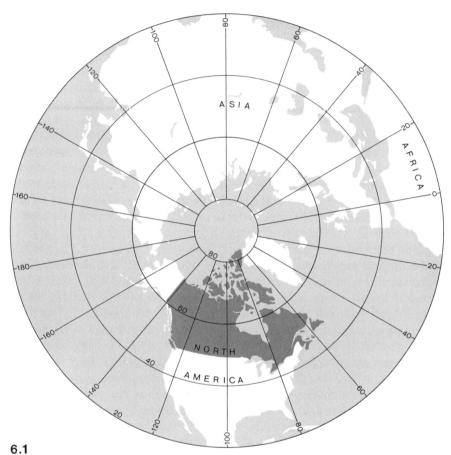

6.1

Canada in the North Polar World

against any possible military overtures against North America and especially the American heartland. Doubtless northern Canada as well as the northern USSR would fill the same role if military action were directed towards the Soviet heartland. Insofar as the North American continent was concerned, the USA regarded itself in the role of protector and there was a clear need to push its front line of warning and defence as far from its national territory as possible. Such defensive installations as the Distant Early Warning (DEW) Line, and the earlier Pine Tree Line were initiated by U.S. defensive self interest[2]; although the northern half of the continent

2 The Canadian government also agreed that Canada must be actively involved

was Canada, this factor was of secondary consequence. The Canadian North was regarded as being in the American sphere, a fact accepted on both sides of the pole. Technological improvements have altered military strategy, so that gradually the DEW Line closed many intermediate stations and the Ballistic Missile Early Warning System (BMEWS) came into operation in 1960. Now the need for warning bases in Canada has all but disappeared and United States defence operates effectively from within the national territory of the USA. The Canadian North at present is only a potential battleground – if necessary. The physical distance across the pole still is the same, but the time required to cross it is very much shorter, and now the great empty spaces of northern Canada – and the northern USSR – are no longer the time/space buffers that provide military insulation.

The Canadian North not only lies between two powerful competing nations, it is unique in that it separates important segments of one of these nations; to reach the state of Alaska by land from 'The Lower Forty-Eight', one must cross Canada. Although a large territory, Alaska is not densely populated, and interest and concern for secure overland connections has evolved in the last few decades. The example of the Alaska Highway, already mentioned, developing as it did during the urgencies of World War II, shows the peculiar symbiosis of U.S. 'need' and financial resources, with Canadian sovereignty over strategically located territory. Other wartime examples exist, some of which have left imprints on the landscape; the Northwest and Northeast Staging routes were airfields and support communications built in Canada with U.S. funds to supply aircraft and other war material to Alaska and USSR in the west, and Europe to the east. The Canol Pipeline from Norman Wells, N.W.T. to Whitehorse, Y.T. was also financed by American funds as a wartime measure. In 1947 and over the next few years joint Canadian–U.S. weather stations were built in the Queen Elizabeth Islands, and other developments such as the DEW Line followed. The catalogue of developments indicates co-operation between the governments of Canada and the United States, but they were not accomplished without friction and discord; many examples could be cited where Canadian rights and feelings were either ignored or taken for granted. The energies and pressures from a large neighbour, no matter how friendly, were often resented; the economic return from massive infusion of U.S capital, on the other hand, was accepted by Canadians as no less than they deserved. Governments on both sides were careful to

with continental defence and, as one of its contributions, Canada built and manned the Mid-Canada Line approximately along the 55th parallel.

protect their own national interest and over the years the relations and arrangements with the United States involving northern Canada have become more a matter of course proceeding in a business-like but cordial fashion.[3]

The importance of position or location of Canada's North in international affairs has for some years been assessed for military reasons. In the recent past the military aspects of strategy have retreated somewhat to allow the economics of resource development to occupy the centre stage of events. Specifically, the discovery of a large pool of oil and natural gas at Prudhoe Bay, Alaska, has quickened interest in the whole of the western Arctic region, both American and Canadian. Exploration and investment have risen sharply; discovery of gas in the Canadian Arctic islands, and oil on the mainland in Canada has given renewed hope for expanding the geographical area of productive sediments. While undoubtedly economically marketable reserves have been proven in Alaska, no oil or gas is reaching a market, and no approved strategies for transportation as yet exist. Many ingredients play a role in the apparent lack of a decision, and without enumerating or assessing them, it is a fact that Alaska, separated as it is from the main market in the lower forty-eight states of the USA must have some transportation link, either through foreign territory or waters (Canada), or via the international high seas from an ice-free Alaswan port. It now seems that oil transportation from Alaska will involve a pipeline; earlier, tanker transportation via the Northwest Passage to the eastern United States was considered and then abandoned after two test journeys and other research. The choice of pipeline routes is between a trans-Alaska line to tidewater, or land connection via the Mackenzie Valley to existing pipelines in Alberta and thence to the United States. The natural gas available in Alaska requires a gas pipeline across Canada. A Canadian route for either oil or gas obviously will require international agreement; the trans-Alaska pipeline and tanker transport to the western USA does not involve Canadian territorial waters, but the fear of oil spills on Canada's west coast highlights a major area of concern for both tanker and pipeline transport – namely the safeguarding of natural ecosystems. Thus the unresolved questions related to petroleum exploitation include the economics of transportation, which is made expensive by the long

3   There are several routes through which exchange takes place, beginning with Canada's Department of External Affairs to the U.S. counterpart, the Secretary of State Department. A variety of joint boards and tribunals exist mostly to co-ordinate northern activities of mutual interest. Currently attempts are being made to minimize overlap in scientific work in the North or to identify areas of northern science which are not sufficiently explored.

distances and engineering problems of the arctic environment, the questions of national sovereignty in route selection, and the new factor of concern for ecological balance of the natural landscape.

The Legacy of European Power in the Canadian North

The external view of the northland of Canada and the question of sovereignty is conditioned by the legacy of European discovery and occupance. Certain distinct intervals of the historical period are dominated by different national interests. In the beginning, the first landfall for Europeans was made by the Norse, and sporadic journeys continued for two hundred years or so after A.D. 1000. What eventually was sketched on maps as the North American continent was, in the fourteenth, fifteenth, and into the sixteenth century, very much a geographical enigma. Concerted efforts to reach the East by going west were focused on specific routes, and the search for the Northwest Passage began about the middle of the sixteenth century. It is fair to say that during these centuries Great Britain and British seamen dominated the search, so that the geographical discovery and mapping of the northern part of North America was mainly a British accomplishment. The mapping process was a long one, ending only in the 1950s after completion of aerial photography of the Arctic islands.

By the beginning of the twentieth century explorers from other nations were turning their attention to the areas north of Canada. National and personal prestige played a role in northern scientific exploration and discovery. Peary of the United States succeeded in being the first to reach the North Pole in 1909, and earlier the Norwegian Otto Sverdrup explored 100,000 square miles of new land in what are now called the Queen Elizabeth Islands. The overwhelming British dominance of northern exploration, therefore, gave way to that of Americans and Norwegians, among others. Questions of sovereignty were not especially contentious when Britain delivered the islands adjacent to the mainland to the young Dominion of Canada in 1880, although the established presence of American whalers in 'Canadian' Arctic waters, and territorial claims by some American explorers were viewed with some agitation. In addition, claims of the 'Sverdrup Islands' by Norway and later Denmark's staking of Ellesmere Island produced positive Canadian responses.

The fact that sovereignty in the Canadian Arctic was, and perhaps still is, regarded by some as at issue implies different points of view, or dispute. The Canadian position and its evolution will be developed later in the chapter. Currently, however, the attitude of the rest of the non-Canadian world to what Canada claims as its own natural territory involves acceptance of the inheritance of British claims by Canada. If, on the other hand, the economic development or 'defensive' military strategies of alien states were to be disrupted by unforeseen events, there might well develop attitudes that challenge Canadian Arctic sovereignty. Two facts give rise to this judgment. First, Canada is not a strong military power fully able to defend by arms its great territorial area, and second, the fact that the northland is almost empty of people, suggests, to some, that it is expendable in military terms.

Canada's North: An Internal View

One would think that a satisfactory way to begin discussing the internal view of Canada's northland would be to define its limits. Although this should not be difficult for Canadians, it clearly is; academics and other northern experts have had serious arguments about the criteria for 'northernness' and a consensus has not yet emerged (see chap. 2). If those who are supposed to know have difficulty, how much less well informed are Canadians generally.

Most Canadians have two images of their northland and make the distinction between 'Arctic' and 'North.' 'Arctic' produces a mental image of snow-covered, treeless lands with ice-filled seas and continuous wind. 'North' probably means uniform trees, many lakes, running water, muskeg, and mosquitoes. Strangely the Arctic is seen in winter, but the North conveys a summer image. The North for Canadians is also a matter of position, one that is distant from their homes in a poleward direction. In fact, the sense of distance towards the pole is heightened by employing an Arctic and polar nomenclature to features and facilities. Thus we may eat at the *Polar Bear Cafe* in Prince Albert, or stay overnight in the *North Star Motel*, or the *Igloo Inn*, or the *Eskimo Hotel* in such towns as Watson Lake, The Pas, or Kapuskasing.[4]

The separate images of Arctic and North as generally perceived are not only environmentally different, but are politically different. The Arctic has the same meaning nationally, and is thought of as a national entity belonging to all Canadians. Because Canada from every place stretches north to the Arctic, we Canadians are different somehow from other North Americans; it is as if the empty land to the north constituted a sort of national security, where an economic future lies in trust, where the pace of development need not be so harassing as life in crowded cities and towns can be; the Arctic is a refuge of unspoiled wilderness. It is relatively easy for all Canadians to feel proprietary towards the Arctic

4 The illustrations are fictional, but the traveller will be able to confirm the suggestion from his own experience.

because it is practically all within the Northwest Territories – at least in the public view – and therefore a ward of the federal government.[5] Furthermore, to demonstrate the all-Canadian attitude to the Arctic, it is only necessary to have problems of ecology, pollution, or sovereignty develop in the Yukon or Northwest Territories to observe a public reaction that is consistent from coast to coast. The present exploration for oil in the Canadian Arctic has stirred differences of opinion, but the debate is a national one, not a provincial or territorial battle. On the other hand, cutting forests or building roads, etc. in northern Saskatchewan or in Northern Ontario will scarcely be noticed by environmentalists in British Columbia or Newfoundland. Developments in the North but within the provinces are usually thought of as provincial affairs.

Whatever division of opinion about the North may exist within Canada, it disappears in the face of outside pressure. The attitude of Canadians about Arctic sovereignty is resolute; any challenge is received with indignation, and any overt threat would be stoutly resisted. The security of the Canadian claim is reflected in the official maps of Canada, beginning first in 1904, which show meridional boundary lines extending along the 141° w and along 60° w to the north pole and enclosing the Canadian 'sector' of the Arctic basin. It creates the impression that Canada 'owns' the land and water in the zone. Although the maps show the sector, no official government legislation makes explicit claim to land *and* water; Canada does claim only the land north of its continental territory. Since the government of Canada became responsible for the island archipelagos, surges of Canadian interest in its Arctic came in response to sovereignty challenges. The Klondike gold rush, the presence of American whalers in the eastern and western Arctic, the Sverdrup explorations, and the Peary expedition to the Pole all prodded Canadian action around the turn of the twentieth century. The Northwest Mounted Police took up permanent stations in the Yukon, on the Beaufort Sea, and in Hudson Bay. World War I distracted northern efforts, but in the 1920s, the Eastern Arctic Patrol became a firmly established annual journey. New police posts and post offices were established as far north as Craig Harbour on Ellesmere Island, the latter in direct response to a Danish claim to the island. Legislation was passed which called for appropriate territorial government, control of fur exports, regulation of scientific activity, protection of

5 The Arctic environment is found in the Yukon Territory, Manitoba, and the Province of Quebec. The Yukon Arctic and the Manitoba Arctic are practically uninhabited, and the Arctic region of Quebec has until recently been under federal administration. The attitude of residents of the Yukon and Northwest Territories to their political aspirations will be discussed later in the chapter.

archaeological sites, and the preservation of game sanctuaries. Gradually by 'effective occupance' and enforced legislation, the Canadian claim to the northern islands emerged unchallenged after the 1930s. Until the post-World War II era, no thought was given to sovereignty claims of the continental shelf, or to the problem of occupied floating ice islands, submarine passages, or, for that matter, territorial waters. The best that can be said for Canada's attitude to the effect of new transportation and military technology is that it is one of vigilance. The law related to pollution of Arctic waters and beaches passed by the Canadian Parliament in 1970 defines standards and responsibilities for foreign vessels operating within 100 miles of the Arctic shoreline. Moreover, Canada does not regard its legislation open to dispute and international arbitration. In other matters, Canada makes every effort to assert the right of consultation and approval for Arctic adventures coming within her legitimate territorial realm.

So far, in considering the internal view of the northland, the unity of attitude by Canadians has been dominant. Such unity of opinion can be a national bond; the 'North' has an effect upon that elusive reality, 'Canadian identity.' That the North has some influence cannot be denied but the importance of the North to Canadians is not easy to measure. There has always been a northern wilderness as settlement spread west in Canada, and with the dominant place of the fur trade in Canadian history, the role of the North in the course of that history is evident. Some Canadian history has been written which gives central play to the northland or the concept of northness. Very often this has meant the conditioning influence of low temperatures, long winters, and snow upon human activity and historical events. The geographers, however, are more likely to think of the northland as space – open and spreading. It is space for the natural world, or space that is like a safety valve for the energies of restless men. It is a zone that in a period of complex society still offers a challenge to man as an individual, one who believes he can succeed with his cunning, an axe, and a rifle. In reality very few northern Canadians have the skills and lore of the *coureurs de bois*, but the knowledge that some have these skills, or more importantly that Canada has a north in which such skills have value, is not only a comfort but a distinction for Canadians. The space of the North is a resource, a wilderness reservoir where people may go to escape briefly the normal, complicated routines of living and refresh themselves in body and spirit; it is a great recreational resource. There is in the north country economic appeal as well as pastoral relief – minerals, trees, and waters may still become economically viable. Frequently the economic future of the North has been portrayed with unjustified optimism, but there is a residual feeling that wealth will one day derive from an untapped source. In this way, the north symbolizes a faith in Canada built both on resources and on human enterprise and added to it are the romantic notions about native Indians and Eskimos, whose ancient ways of living are classic examples of man in harmony with nature. Because it is not generally appreciated how much this image has changed, the noble native remains one of the enduring symbols of the northland of Canada.

The Jurisdictional Evolution of the North
For European man, jurisdiction over territory is fundamental; when people with European cultural roots came and took dominion of the new world, the map became strewn with lines or boundaries deemed necessary to define spheres of authority. Before the advent of European man in what is now the Canadian North there was territoriality in which the margins of territory were of concern only to groups of people living on either side of a boundary who had reason to respect one another. European exploration on the other hand was determined to learn about and know of all existing land; it continued the drive to discover and divide up the world. Many competing nations accepted the challenge of exploration, made discoveries, and claimed new land, and by defining territory brought boundaries to the maps. The story of the evolution of boundaries in Canada has been well told (Nicholson 1954). It may be reviewed by examining the plates of an historical atlas which traditionally have had similar format and orientation; as presented, the maps have north at the 'top' and boundary changes appear to move westward with time and the spread of settlement from shore to shore. Seldom have there been attempts to alter this way of looking at boundary evolution.

The discovery, followed by competitive exploration, of North America at first involved Dutch, French, and British expeditions. In short order Britain and France were the main protagonists, the former established on the Atlantic coast of what is now the United States, and the latter along the St Lawrence River. Since the origin of exploration was in western Europe, it is illuminating to illustrate what the emerging coastline of North America looked like from say the western shore of Britain (Figure 6.2). Two deep openings into the heart of the continent exist; one was the St Lawrence under French control, and a second, and deeper, was Hudson Bay. By way of the Bay, it was possible to sail into the heartland of the continent, a locational advantage taken by the British. The fur resources, particularly beaver, in the hinterland of the Bay sustained interest in the region and became the foundation of the commercial empire staked out on the shores of the northern sea. In some ways, this central and dominant position, which survived an early French challenge, might well have fore-

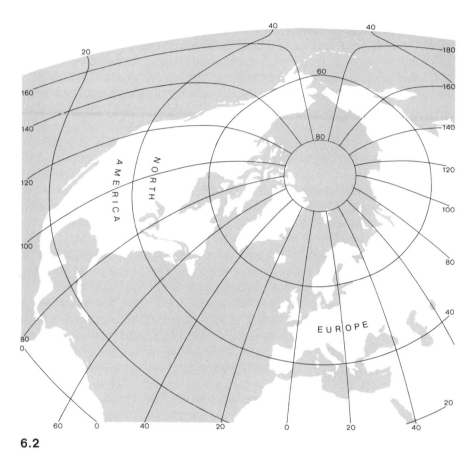

6.2

North America Seen from Britain

told the successful spread of the British heritage over northern North America. Thus, the first British boundary in what is now Canada defined the Charter Territory of the Hudson's Bay Company in 1670, and in terms of area it was a massive bite out of the northern part of the continent. In time, fur trade competition and amalgamation with competitors permitted the Company to extend its commercial government beyond the Charter domain to take in most of the boreal lands of North America and hold it under central control for two hundred years.

At great distances from the Bay on the outer margins of the Company's lands, settlement flourished where the soil and climate permitted the establishment of basic agriculture. Populations grew, governments evolved, and provinces in time linked together, so that new territorial jurisdictions were carved from the edges of the older, larger core. The great commercial presence of the Hudson's Bay Company shrank inward towards the Bay as jurisdictional nibbling moved from east to west to north in a great flanking action.

The chronology of territorial evolution is not matched by the evolution of government that might be expected with passing time. For example, Rupert's Land of the Hudson's Bay Company was the first major territorial definition, and yet two hundred years later its government was essentially the same as it was in the beginning. Around the margins of this large territory other provinces were created, flourished, and evolved in governmental form. What, of course, was happening was the greater insistence of geography taking pre-eminence over history; in the south the 'gradient of nature' was more favourable to agriculture, subsequent settlement, and population growth than it was in the North. As population increased and wealth grew, there also grew a demand to participate in and accept responsibility for government. In time, the most suitable land for settlement was pre-empted and the single jurisdiction with which European government of the North began gave way to multiple government.

The pattern of governmental growth and territorial division started with Rupert's Land, which was defined by a drainage divide marking off those lands that contributed streams to Hudson Bay and Hudson Strait (Figure 6.3). The organization of territory in eastern North America did not infringe that grant, but after the Treaty of Paris (1763), which gave French colonies over to British rule, and especially after the Treaty of Versailles (1783), which recognized the United States of America, two provinces of Upper and Lower Canada were fitted like a jig-saw next to Rupert's Land in the south and east. The country west of Upper Canada seemed wide open, and under the lead of the North West Company, fur traders entered and pursued exploration westward and northward. The amalgamation of the two fur trading companies under the name of the Hudson's Bay Company in 1821 re-established the fur monopoly, and the North Western Territory – essentially the land of Arctic drainages – joined Rupert's Land under Company control. Furthermore, the Company spread across the Great Divide to extend its control to the Pacific drainage. Here conflict with the Americans to the south and Russia to the north led to treaty negotiations and boundary definition. In 1825 agreement with Russia limited the westward spread of British traders to 141° w, the present boundary between the Yukon Territory and Alaska, and the northward spread up the coast to 54° 40′ N, the southern limit of Alaska's panhandle. Much later, in 1846, agreement with the United States split the Oregon Terri-

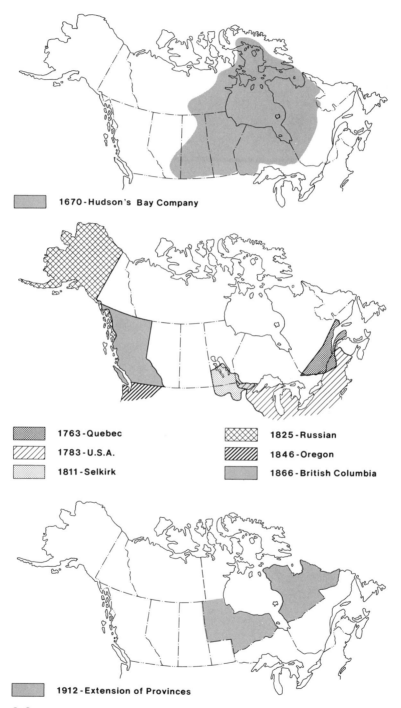

1763 - Quebec	1825 - Russian
1783 - U.S.A.	1846 - Oregon
1811 - Selkirk	1866 - British Columbia

1670 - Hudson's Bay Company

1912 - Extension of Provinces

6.3
Selected Canadian Boundary Factors

tory, and the 49th parallel was accepted as the boundary between American authority and British North America. This British realm was for the most part the preserve of the fur trader, and, of course, the indigenous people. Settlement, however, was destined to develop in the west, with the Selkirk Colony at Red River being the first. After its beginning in 1811 the growth of the colony was integrated to the needs of the Hudson's Bay Company and may be said to have been part of the Company operation. Farther west along the Fraser River the discovery of gold produced a great influx of people fresh from the California rush. The need for territorial reorganization and firm government was quickly apparent and the Hudson's Bay Company Colony of Vancouver Island became the Crown Colony of Vancouver Island. At the same time the colony of British Columbia was established on the mainland in 1858, with James Douglas the governor of both colonies. The two were joined in 1866 with the boundaries then described being practically the same today.

The Canadian Confederation of 1867 started the integration of provinces and gave purpose and direction to the established trend in westward settlement. Successful negotiations added two new provinces – Manitoba, the old Red River Settlement; and British Columbia, the former colony. In these acts, Great Britain launched its first self-governing Dominion, and promptly delivered half a continent into the hands of a fledgling government. It did so by assisting in the transfer of Rupert's Land from the Hudson's Bay Company to Canada and adding the North Western Territories, once leased to the Bay, so that by 1870 one vast tract, the Northwest Territories (which included the Yukon), came under the control of Canada. Furthermore, the Arctic islands became Canadian in 1880 by act of the Westminster Parliament.

In the period from 1870 until 1912 there was a parade of territories, districts and provinces that were created, altered, absorbed, and redefined by multiple boundary changes. The boundary and administrative changes were all in response to growing settlement and, although the details of the changes are unimportant here, they resulted in the present montage of provinces extending from coast to coast. Once the east–west drive was completed, there came the move for northward manifestations of destiny. Alberta, Saskatchewan, and Manitoba adopted the 60th parallel for a northern boundary. By 1912 both Ontario and Quebec took parts of Rupert's Land to extend their domains to Hudson Bay and Hudson Strait. Thus the present political pattern, unchanged since 1912, shows the federal government left with exclusive control over a fraction of the former grand domain – the Yukon Territory, which flourished and faded, and the residual Northwest Territories.

Government of the Canadian North

The evolution of boundaries and designation of territories, districts, and provinces tells very little about how the land is governed. Canada is a federal state within which provinces accept responsibilities and have powers that apply to the provincial realm, and at the federal level, a central government has authority over nationwide questions. The division of authority is enacted in law but questioned by continual re-interpretation. The political divisions on the map of Canada tend to suggest provincial supremacy within the provinces, when in fact the federal government has many responsibilities that cut across provincial boundaries. Moreover, the federal government controls the northern Territories.

An example of federal responsibility that transgresses provincial limits is the government of the Indian population. As an historical legacy, all programs related to Indians, as legally defined, are federal ones, and include providing for their health, education, and welfare. It might be argued that the Indian population tends to be Canada's northern population, since the percentage of Indians in the total population tends to increase as one proceeds north.[6] As the Indians are well represented in areas where major modern developments have not yet taken place, the population depends more upon federal government programs, even though the locale may be within provincial bounds. The Eskimos, the other major indigenous group in Canada, are also federal wards. The Eskimos do not have specific legal arrangements with any government in Canada, unlike the Indians who have their signed treaties. They are, however, in receipt of federal health, education, and welfare arrangements. Eskimos in northern Manitoba and in Arctic Quebec were totally under federal supervision until a few years ago. Labrador Eskimos only became Canadians with the 1949 Confederation of Newfoundland, but the programs applicable to other Canadian Eskimos were made available in Labrador through grants administered by the province.

The uniformity of governmental control of native aboriginal people of Canada's North which existed in the 1950s is now in a state of change. The Province of Quebec is seeking to extend provincial services and jurisdiction to all people within the provincial realm, including Indians and Eskimos. The easement from one governmental authority to another, although negotiated and gradual, is not without difficulty. The process is still continuing and perhaps the fundamental difference, for the Eskimos at least, is the fact that federal administration and education was conducted in English, but now the provincial administration is introducing

6 Many Indians live in southern Canada, with increasing numbers settling in the cities. But in the North they seem more dominant because of fewer whites.

the French language. In addition, there is a natural concern, on the part of the natives, for the quality of such services as health and education when the provincial authority takes over – a basic apprehension about the unknown. Within other provincial jurisdictions where aboriginal people reside, the full program of federal benefits and controls applies pursuant to the obligations of treaties signed. Indian health, welfare, and education are the main responsibilities, but programs intended to promote economic stability and progress among natives are also federally sponsored.[7] It has been noted that the Territories do not have the same degree of responsible government found in the provinces. They are, as yet, under the ultimate control of the central government. These regions, sparsely populated but growing, are waiting for a stronger economic future. The Yukon Territory, marked out as it was in 1898 during the height of the Klondike gold rush, briefly experienced the population size and wealth to press for and receive government reflecting a measure of local participation. Legislation provided a Council headed by an Ottawa-appointed Commissioner which, within a few years, became wholly elected with its own speaker. Economic depression later provoked changes in the number of councillors and at one point threatened to eliminate them altogether. But better times returned and a Council of seven members now sits with the Commissioner to make governmental decisions in all areas excepting natural resources, which are still controlled by Ottawa. The Commissioner of the Territory has executive power, particularly since Ottawa is still the main source of financial support and he administers federal funds for the Yukon. Nevertheless, a territorial civil service is well established and government of the Yukon is located for the most part in the Territory, with the capital at Whitehorse. This 'government at home' has not compensated totally for the distant Ottawa budget control, and with his traditional independence the Yukoner is still working for completely responsible government like that of the other provinces of Canada. The Yukon Territory is also a federal electoral riding, and has returned a member to the federal Parliament since 1902.

The Northwest Territories in some way fulfils the Biblical prophecy of 'the first shall be last.' The territorial area was delineated early, then cannibalized, so the present Territories, what is left, are only now slowly working towards the political maturity of the rest of Canada. Like the

7 It would be possible to show how many activities of the federal government carried out within any or all of the ten provinces and two territories that do not clash with provincial authority. For example, the Department of the Environment operates all weather stations; the Geological Survey of Canada may have field operations anywhere in the country; the federal courts are available to all Canadians.

Yukon with its gold rush, the first improvement in government of the Northwest Territories was in response to a resource boom – the discovery of oil at Norman Wells in 1921. The provision of government by a Commissioner and Council, similar to that of the Yukon, was made in 1905, but the Territories themselves were further truncated in 1912 when Quebec, Ontario, and Manitoba were 'completed' by the annexation of all mainland east, south, and west of Hudson Bay, at least north to the 60th parallel. During this time the Commissioner alone, resident in Ottawa, administered the whole of the Northwest Territories. After 1921 four councillors were appointed to advise the Commissioner. Progress towards local participation in territorial government was slow mainly because the population was composed largely of native Indians and Eskimos and Métis. At the time they were unaware of the need or workings of government and instead accepted advice and direction from the local white authority, be he priest, trader, or policeman. The mining rush at Yellowknife during the 1930s resulted in producing mines, bringing a stable growth in the white population which, in turn, provoked changes in government. World War II intervened, but after it, the Council of the Northwest Territories appointed its first local member. During the last twenty years evolution of the Council has brought about changes in its members and composition, so that the federal civil service element strongly represented in earlier days has been phased out; now only the Commissioner and Deputy Commissioner are civil servants. Altogether, in addition to the Commissioner and Deputy Commissioner, the Council comprises ten elected members representing constituencies in the Territories, plus three appointed members from outside the Territories.

Significant changes in government occurred following the 1966 report of an Advisory Commissioner re Development in the N.W.T. Following its recommendations, the capital moved from Fort Smith to Yellowknife almost immediately, with the Commissioner resident there. During 1968 and 1969 the Territorial government gradually developed its own administrative machinery, including civil service, to take over most of the federally administered programs. In the process, many federal civil servants transferred to the Territorial government, accepting responsibility for directing industrial development, social development, education, local government, public works, legal services, etc. Like the Yukon, however, the natural resources, including land, are within the exclusive purview of Ottawa. Thus progress is being made towards independent and representative control of government in the Northwest Territories comparable to that in the provinces of Canada. The people of the Northwest Territories have had representation in the federal Parliament since 1952 when the constituency of Mackenzie was created. Before that, for a brief period, some Mackenzie residents were able to vote for the Yukon member. Not until 1962, however, did the federal franchise become universal, and by recent amendment the voting age has been lowered to 19 years. Presently one member is returned to Parliament.

Political Prospects

It seems certain that continuing economic and social developments in the Canadian North will have political implications on both the international and national scene. In both cases this region is a frontier. So long as world politics are dominated by both the United States of America and the Union of Soviet Socialist Republics, and as long as these powers have unresolved differences, the strategic location of northern Canada geographically between the two means that the north country lies open to developments in military strategy and technology. The terrain, climate, and distances all must figure in plans for defence preparedness. Canada herself, in keeping with her own sense of destiny and sovereignty has recently augmented the Canadian military presence in the North by a program of air surveillance, and ground forces that have been especially designated and are being trained for arctic military activity. In the same way that Canada is asserting her own claims and controls of the military future of the North, she is prepared to guide the economic future of the vast area. Northern resources until recently were the traditional ones – fur, forests, and metalliferous ores. With the exceptions of placer gold in the Klondike and the wartime activities in the 1940s, most development did not cause great rushes of capital and people to the region. Now, however, the oil and gas prospects in the western Arctic are having major economic consequences. The pressures to bring these new resources to market face the necessity that it be accomplished in an orderly way to give benefit to the people of the North, and cause minimum disturbance to the natural landscape. Doubtless technological advances in northern engineering and transportation will need to accompany resource development, and Canada is evolving international and national policies to make secure her territorial integrity. Canadian activity in the North has never been greater, encompassing a full range of social, scientific, engineering, and administrative programs. If doubts exist about the claims of Canadian sovereignty, they are certainly not in the minds of Canadians who, through their government, are accepting full responsibility for the future of their northland.

The pace of change in the society of the Canadian North has quickened greatly in the last decade. Steady progress is being made in lifting the level of basic social services for the whole of the northland's population. In particular, this means assisting the native people through health, housing, education, and social development programs to play a stronger role in their own destiny. Now native leadership, sometimes based on the institutionalized tribal or band organization and sometimes based on new native associations, has become vocal and firm. For the first time native opinions and advice have political repercussions, with local politicians and governments responding. Although the system of government administrators still operates in the Northwest Territories, several examples of devolving responsibility onto locally elected councils or boards exist. Municipal government has been started, and school district administration begun – all signs of a brighter political future.

The white population of the North has until recently been outnumbered by the natives. The population of the Northwest Territories is presently 42 per cent non-native and the Yukon is 85 per cent non-native; taken together, 60 per cent are not counted as Indians or Eskimos. Many whites are resident northerners of long standing who regard the North as their permanent homes. Government employees, until recently, tended to be resident for short periods of time, but now that the N.W.T. territorial government responsibilities have increased, more civil servants will have longer northern careers. These people have been influential for a long time in the course of northern government. But this too is changing as the native people develop and make known independent political viewpoints. Thus there is a challenge in future northern politics; it is a challenge to the whites to accept with grace and goodwill the consequences of native participation in future decisions, and a challenge to the native community to face the hard realities of working for the well-being of all northerners, themselves included, within a social system unlike anything in their heritage. That the challenge will be met is not in question. The only way open is the road to success, and it is the first step towards the evolution of total responsibility in government.

7 The Future of Northern Canada

WILLIAM C. WONDERS

In many ways the future of the North is the future of Canada. Within a nation of immense size and relatively small population the North contributes the largest part of that size and at the same time the smallest numbers of people. Canada has been long accustomed to the problems of knitting together on a continental scale the distinctive segments of its southern margin. It is now confronted with a north–south dimension of equal magnitude. If modern technology has rendered the physical mastery of its space easier than when the southern links were forged a hundred years ago, it is not without problems and costs. Yet these problems and costs must be surmounted.

Formerly, geographic isolation both nationally and internationally, from centres of political and economic power, permitted the North to move at a more leisurely pace. Canada, inheriting rather than seeking much of it, was nonetheless prepared to add the North to her political map. Other nations in the main showed even less interest in it, so that Canadian ownership of this vast area was possible with minimum responsibilities. World War II and the subsequent years changed all this. The past 30 years have seen far greater change than the preceding 300 years. In an era suddenly aware of shrunken global dimensions and resources, of the close interdependence in the 'world island,' the Canadian North no longer is isolated, nationally or internationally. The northerner still refers to people and events 'outside,' reflecting his sense of isolation from the bulk of Canadians. At the same time he increasingly expects to receive his southern metropolitan area newspaper only a day or two late, rather than after a delay of weeks, months, or even years as in past decades. Problems once troublesome only in that same 'outside' world now are encountered in the North as well. The North also has contributed certain problems distinctive to itself. Several of these – economic, social, political – have been pointed out in specific contexts in the previous chapters in this volume.

It is perhaps foolhardy for a geographer to predict how future historians and political scientists will evaluate the contributions of a nation. Yet one of the most distinctive features of Canada is its northern situation. It is reasonable to expect, therefore, that in the final analysis the North can be expected to figure prominently in any such evaluation – what has the North meant for Canada as a nation, how well has Canada integrated this huge area into its national framework, how successful has Canada been in dealing with the many formidable problems which the North contributes along with its assets?

In large part the answers to such questions will be decided by two factors or combination of factors: the attitudes of Canadians towards the North and external pressures bearing upon it (or 'internal' and 'external,' to repeat Stager's phraseology).

ATTITUDES TOWARDS THE NORTH

To the Present

Traditionally the North has been regarded as a vast warehouse to be exploited vigorously and in some cases ruthlessly, to provide riches for the outside world. Whether the resources be whales, furs, minerals, or forest products, the main objective overall has been to extract the product for the maximum profit of individuals living far removed from the region. To this end transportation services have been extended into the North along with other improvements. However, it can not be denied that all too often the inheritance, once the resource was exhausted, was dereliction both physical and social. There are cases where the 'exploiters' have demonstrated responsibility – where trading posts have continued to serve trapping communities after the catch or the fur price economically would not warrant it, or where some pulp and paper mills on the southern margins of the region have aimed at a long-term presence – but such cases are exceptional in the total northern scene.

Since quick wealth was the goal, the approach was to find the resource, exploit it, and either move on to the next supply or return 'outside' if the profit was sufficient. Where a renewable resource was involved conservation was rarely considered and then usually only as a last resort. The legendary frontier of dazzling weath potential so beloved in the American scene shifted to the North as the West somewhat reluctantly settled into a more comfortable routine. The vastness of the North still permitted the illusion of unlimited resources with a corresponding callousness towards what was left behind once it had served its purpose.

Attitudes towards the indigenous peoples of the North have varied with time. Initially, in the earliest period of white arrival and exploration, the natives were regarded perhaps as curiosities more than anything. Indeed, such attitudes towards the Eskimos persisted until the late nineteenth century at least. Early, however, in the case of the Indians and later for the Eskimos, they were recognized as potentially useful contributors to the resource extraction process. Native people played an indispensable role in early water transportation services and in whaling and trapping. As transportation became more sophisticated, however, and as whaling and more recently trapping became relatively unimportant economically, the role of the native inhabitant also changed. From being a 'participant' (albeit a humble one) in the economic life of the North, he found himself increasingly an outside observer. Bewildered that his traditional skills were no longer of value and at the same time increasingly bound to the white man's settlements and way of life, the native Northerner often lapsed into the self-destructive role of 'hanger-on.' In the eyes of the 'outsiders' he became a liability of the area – at worst a nuisance for the exploiter, at best an object of charity to be attended to first by the church and more recently by government.

For the white incomers the North has been a place in which hopefully to strike it rich. Once wealth was acquired, whether it was enough to provide generously for the rest of an individual's life or only sufficient to enable him to buy a farm or home 'outside,' the traditional pattern has been to leave the area. Until very recently the North has never been regarded as a permanent place of residence by the white incomer (with perhaps some exceptions in its south-central sectors). Most white 'Northerners' considered themselves temporary residents only. They also have been mainly a male population, the women waiting at home for the men to return once sufficient wealth was accumulated. Transients make up a considerable percentage of the population, drifting in to seek employment; but even if it is found, often moving on within a short time.

In view of such conditions and attitudes, it is scarcely surprising that the northern settlements of the white incomers have been notably lacking in elements of permanency and of beauty. Shelter could be rudimentary and makeshift since the white inhabitant was only there for as short a time as possible and anything would do in the interval. Indeed, the presence of amenities beyond the basic is all the more remarkable in the northern setting – the Palace Grand Theatre of Dawson, for example. In turn, the camplike nature of so many northern settlements in the past has contributed to the difficulty of instilling a resident attitude and responsibility in the white incomer. Yet there have been individuals who have spent most of their lives in the North. Whereas 'outsiders' tend to attach them-

selves to a particular place, long-time white Northerners have more charac-
teristically attached themselves to the larger region, but often have moved
frequently within it.

In the Present

Many of the attitudes outlined above still persist. The primary role of the
North in the minds of most Canadians is undoubtedly to provide a resource base for the rest of the country. This now centres mainly upon the
mineral wealth of the region. The distinctive physical characteristics of
the North which Bird has set out pose major problems, but modern technology has progressed to the point where they can be overcome, as Marsden makes clear in connection with transportation. The result is the impressive mining industry of today which has been the major factor in the
rapid changes which have occurred in the North during the past thirty
years. Impressive though these have been, they really are a continuation
of the same attitudes that have prevailed in the past, and though tempered
now by such phrases as 'pollution control,' 'social responsibility,' etc., the
prevalent attitude still, by individuals, corporations, and governments, is
'what can the area contribute economically for our benefit' (Judd 1969)?
Tough reminds us that all mines ultimately must reach the end of their ore
– and the result remains the same today as yesterday.

Initially enunciated as a political slogan, 'northern development' in recent years has drawn enthusiastic support from all Canadians and now is
an accepted policy of all levels of government (see Mills [1971] for a
recent statement of federal government policies). Interpretation of what
constitutes 'northern development' or more specifically 'responsible' northern development still reflects considerable variation from one part of the
nation to another and from one segment of population to another. Con-
flicts between conservation groups and developers, between native residents and incomers, already have introduced unprecedented controversy
in the case of Alaskan oil and gas which has had repercussions in northern
Canada. Concern over potential environmental catastrophe in the Canadian Arctic, for example, prompted the Canadian government to enunciate
firm policy statements of wide-reaching international ramifications (Beesley 1971). Similar concern is forcing oil and gas and mining companies to
take very great precautions against environmental damage in their exploration and production, even to the point where some claim it may deter
such operations entirely.

Recent technological mastery of many of the problems of the North
(admittedly at considerable cost) has made it possible for Northerners
to share with fellow Canadians a near-instantaneous awareness of wider

news and social currents. A prospector in a remote bush camp listens on his radio to a National Hockey League playoff game taking place thousands of miles away, while his wife in a northern town studies the latest fashions in a television program from the capitals of Europe. Young people turn out dutifully to purchase in what used to be a simple fur-trading post the same pop record that their peers are listening to with dedicated concentration in Montreal, Toronto, or Vancouver.

The same social services enjoyed by southern Canadians are now demanded and in large measure received by the northern residents. In the process the rights of the native Northerner particularly are being recognized. In recent years strenuous efforts have been made by governments to provide every educational opportunity for the young people – indeed perhaps better opportunities and facilities than are available in some of the long-settled but economically deprived areas of southern Canada. At the same time it must be conceded that the position of the middle-aged or older northern native person all too often remains in limbo.

Transportation and communication improvements which have played a large part in making possible this 'modern North' also have imparted a strong north–south internal regionalization to the area, as Marsden, Bone, and Hamelin have noted. The northward extension of service facilities by a relatively few large southern metropolitan centres offers little opportunity for any significant northern urban challengers.

The southern provinces, with the exception of the Maritimes, now have discovered that their boundaries take in part of the North. For a variety of reasons all have recently taken an increased interest in the North, though the variety of ways in which they define it contributes in no small degree to that confusion in terminology to which Hamelin alludes. Among all three so-called Prairie Provinces for example, royal commissions or special research studies have gone into the conditions and prospects of their Norths, special bodies have been established to develop them (e.g. Northern Alberta Development Council), and research institutes have been established in each of the senior universities in each province.[1]

Regrettably, the North has been involved in the current national political debate or contest in Canada wherein the provinces have been pressing their claims vigorously, usually at the expense of the fedeal government. In some cases northern problems are being unnecesarily complicated by the historical accident of political boundaries. Usually defined on an arbitrary basis, they often bear little relationship to geographic realities. In

1   The Boreal Institute at the University of Alberta, Edmonton; The Institute for Northern Studies at the Saskatoon Campus of the University of Saskatchewan; the Center for Settlement Studies at the University of Manitoba, Winnipeg.

Table 7.1 Resource revenue and expenditures, Northwest Territories ($000)

Year	Total resource expenditures	Total 'provincial-type' resource expenditures	Total 'provincial-type' resource revenue
1965	12,095	9,117	7,165
1966	11,748	8,244	2,482
1967	17,271	12,172	2,544
1968	16,134	11,154	3,112
1969	24,603	19,374	3,371
Total	81,851	59,962	18,674

Source: Canada, Dept. of Indian Affairs and Northern Development.

Table 7.2 Resource revenue and expenditures, Yukon Territory ($000)

Year	Total resource expenditures	Total 'provincial-type' resource expenditures	Total 'provincial-type' resource revenue
1965	7,314	6,044	469
1966	8,462	7,133	601
1967	11,227	9,978	589
1968	18,825	17,585	772
1969	10,925	9,726	1,767
Total	62,753	50,465	4,198

Source: Canada, Dept. of Indian Affairs and Northern Development.

our present era, however, unnecessary delay and cost are often encountered in the implementation of what otherwise is not a serious problem for our technology and resources (Wonders 1970). The current discussions on construction of a road to serve Ft Smith, N.W.T., Ft Chipewyan, Alberta, and Uranium City, Saskatchewan, is a case in point.

As northerners have become increasingly similar to other Canadians in way of life and points of view there have been increasing demands, at least by a segment of them, for greater political autonomy – for the conversion of the northern territories into provinces. An Advisory Commission on the Development of Government in the Northwest Territories brought down a report in 1966 and since then, as Stager has noted, various political changes have been implemented both in the Northwest Territories and in the Yukon Territory. Yet with so small a population still involved in such vast areas, and including such a significant number of native peoples, the problems will not be solved by provincial status alone. Tables 7.1 and 7.2 illustrate the marked discrepancies which still persist in expenditures and revenue on resources alone in recent years. In major policy statements made in Yellowknife and in Whitehorse in November 1969, the Minister of Indian Affairs and Northern Development indicated that the federal government would not be stampeded into what it considered premature change of the northern territories into provinces (Chrétien 1969).

In the Future
There is little to indicate that most Canadians see the future economic role of the North as differing much from its role today. Scientific knowledge has made us highly sceptical of many of the wildly optimistic claims of the past, and improved transportation, changed social values, and higher income have actually reduced some limited resource development (e.g. agriculture) in the area. While much of it is forested, trees often can be grown more economically in milder latitudes, so that forest development, even on its southern margins, comes slowly.

Today most economic development in the North centres on mining, and it is expected that it will continue to be so in the future. This is the theme that emerges from the plethora of northern development conferences which have erupted across Canada over the past decade. The scale of operations in such developments will continue to increase, with both the benefits (financial, stability) and the risks (environmental) involved. Developments in the Labrador iron fields and the Anvil lead–zinc project in the Yukon give some measure of what is likely to come. Increasing Canadian nationalism, however, is reflected in the growing pressure for more processing of minerals within Canada, which would be particularly beneficial to the narrowly specialized northern economy if such facilities were located there.

Currently the great unknown in the mineral future of northern Canada is the oil and gas factor. The near-frantic activity in the exploration phase which followed the Prudhoe Bay discovery in Arctic Alaska continues unabated in the Canadian Arctic, to the local benefit chiefly of northern transportation operators, expediters, and mechanics. While commercial discoveries and exploitation would be highly beneficial for northern resource income, it should be kept in mind that the oil and gas industry is a highly automated one and, following the initial construction phase, maintenance personnel would be minimal.

The very emptiness of the North, so long a handicap for it, already is being re-appraised by southern Canadians and particularly by Americans still farther south. Confronted with an increasingly congested, polluted environment at home, these people look longingly to the North as a means of escape, even if only a temporary one. The recreation and sports attractions of the North, moreover, are now within reach of more and more southerners via aircraft and road extensions. There has been a significant increase in sports and recreation facilities on a commercial basis in the North and potentially this offers a major area for future development; it also has the advantage of widening the northern economic base with almost no associated disadvantages.

Another potential northern resource of a much more controversial nature is the fresh water which makes up such a large percentage of the area. Already several schemes have been suggested to divert northern water southwards to the United States. The proponents view such suggestions as opportunities to capitalize on an underutilized northern resource; the opponents as still further evidence of the exploiters' callous disregard for the environment and for the North.

Despite significant differences within the North, there still are greater overriding similarities which give it cohesiveness and regional identity despite the superimposed artificial political boundaries. Regrettably, political pronouncements for momentary publicity may have unforeseen repercussions. The suggestion that British Columbia extend its boundaries northward to the Arctic Ocean (made in 1968) or the casual extension northward of 'roads to resources' as an election idea are examples. An action for the political and economic advantage of one outside area may not be the most desirable for the North or the nation as a whole.

The opportunity which the North provides for an unprecedented vast master plan of development is a concept which has been appreciated by a minority of Canadians to date. Several presidents of the Canadian Association of Geographers have touched on such an idea in varying degrees in their presidential addresses (e.g. Lloyd 1959; Bird 1960; Wonders 1962; Hare 1964). Recently it was more fully developed and widely publicized as the 'Mid-Canada Development Corridor' (Acres 1967), which includes a broad arc across Canada's Middle North, including the 'most positive elements' for potential development. To implement such a project, its originator, R. Rohmer, suggests the establishment of a Corporation 'in which the provincial, territorial and federal governments are equal partners as to control and financing' (Rohmer 1970, p. 105).

The opportunities for most efficient and beneficial planning which such truly regional or national planning provide must surely outweigh local factional considerations. It should prevent the repetition of such ecological disasters as the Bennett Dam on the Peace River, or at least force a proper evaluation of projects involving the wider region, with adequate compensation for those adversely affected. We can no longer afford or tolerate the selfish exploitation of the past. Moreover, all Canadian taxpayers have been contributing to northern development, so why should not all parts of Canada join with northern residents in its future instead of perpetuating further political subdivision of this large area. Existing provincial boun-

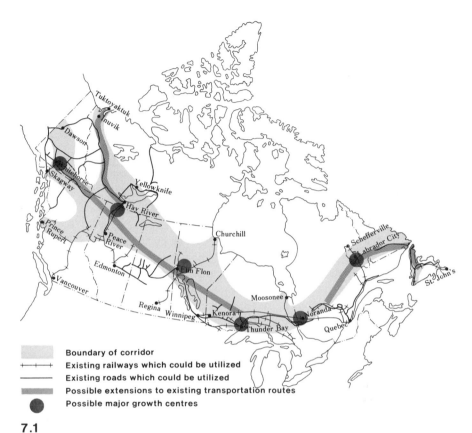

Boundary of corridor
+—+—+ Existing railways which could be utilized
——— Existing roads which could be utilized
▬▬▬ Possible extensions to existing transportation routes
● Possible major growth centres

7.1

Mid-Canada Development Corridor

(Source: Acres Limited)

daries have divided the nation in recent years as much as they have united it. Canadians should not follow doggedly a nineteenth century political frame-of-mind towards their frontier areas. If they or their leaders have enough imagination, the North offers them not only wealth and problems but also the opportunity to contribute something unique and positive to future generations.

EXTERNAL PRESSURES ON THE CANADIAN NORTH

Stager and Tough have pointed out many of the external pressures which have applied in the past and still apply to the Canadian North. They are both political and economic. Until World War II they were not too serious – Danish, Norwegian, and American 'flurries' in the Arctic, though American attitudes in the Yukon and in the Alaskan Panhandle left a bitterness among many Canadians.

World War II and the increasing range of aircraft made Canadians aware of their northern dimensions for the first time. The North East Staging Route, the North West Staging Route, the Alaska Highway, the Canol Project saw Americans in the wartime emergency transform large areas of the Canadian North at a pace which left the locals breathless. It has never been the same since. The postwar 'Cold War' between the world's two superpowers made northern Canada an even more critical area. Such expensive and highly complex projects as the Joint Arctic Weather Stations and the DEW Line were implemented with minimal, if any, concern for Canadian political sensitivities and as a side effect resulted in the final and complete disruption of the few Eskimo people still living off the land. No illusions were left that in a serious 'emergency' Canada could really control policies involving her North. It should be conceded, of course, that benefits (chiefly in transportation and communication) often accompanied these emergencies, but a price was paid.

In recent years economic pressures have been reflected chiefly in the demand for the mineral resources of the Canadian North. Most of these flow to the United States, but Japan and Germany also are involved, so that Canada is tied ever more tightly to continental and in lesser degree to world markets. Income and social benefits to northern Canadians have accompanied this mineral development. Nonetheless, with the overwhelming majority of such companies foreign-controlled, there is real concern that the future of the region and of its inhabitants is decided not just 'outside' but abroad. Hence, while resource development is welcomed, disquiet is noteworthy, particularly among the young. Even if a consensus is reached among Canadians in their attitudes towards the North and on the desirable future for it, there is growing disquiet about their ability to direct this in view of the economic facts of the situation. Hopefully, a solution will be found to maintain and increase development with national interests adequately guaranteed.

Magnificent and miserable, exhilarating and depressing, beautiful and ugly – the North is all these and more. When all is said and done, it is the North that imparts to Canada its most distinctive flavour. With its wealth and promise, the North provides us with challenges of corresponding magnitude. During the past 30 years it has been knit into the Canadian fabric to an unprecedented degree. Undoubtedly, the future will see it playing a more and more important role in the life of the nation, becoming more and more familiar both to Canadians and to visitors to this country.

References

Acres Research and Planning Ltd. (*c.* 1967) *Mid-Canada Development Corridor – a Concept* (Toronto)

Andrews, J.T., 1970 A geomorphological study of post-glacial uplift with particular reference to arctic Canada, *Inst. Brit. Geogr. Spec. Pub*, 2: 156

Bandeen, R.A., 1969 Railways in Northern resource development, *in* B.F. Sater (ed.), *Arctic and Middle North Transportation*, 145–7

Battelle Memorial Institute, 1961 *Transport Requirements for the Growth of Northwest North America* (Columbus, Ohio [A report for the Alaska International Rail & Highway Commission])

Beals, C.S. (ed.) 1968 *Science, History and Hudson Bay* (Queen's Printer, Ottawa), 2 vols.

Beesley, J.A., 1971 Rights and responsibilities of Arctic coastal states: the Canadian view, *Arctic Circular*, XXII, 2: 98–110

Biays, P., 1964 *Les marges de l'oekoumène dans l'Est du Canada* (Québec): 762

Bird, J.B., 1960 The scenery of central and southern Arctic Canada, *Can. Geogr.*, 15: 1–11

— 1967 *The Physiography of Arctic Canada* (Baltimore)

Bladen, V.W. (ed.), 1962 *Canadian Population and Northern Colonization* (Toronto)

Boreal Institute, University of Alberta, 1968 *Proc. Symp. on the implications of Northern mineral resources management for human development* (19th Alaskan Science Conference), Boreal Inst. *Occas. Publ.* 5 (Edmonton)

Brochu, M., 1965 Présentation et commentaires de cartes sur le Nouveau-Québec, *L'Actualité économique*, 40, 4: 691–759

Brooks, D.B., G.W. Tough and W. Keith Buck, 1970 *Conservation of Mineral and Environmental Resources*, Mineral Resources Branch, Information Bull. MR 109 (Information Canada, Ottawa)

Brown, R.J.E., 1970 *Permafrost in Canada* (Toronto)

Buck, W. Keith, 1970 *Factors Influencing the Mineral Economy of Canada*, Mineral Resources Branch, Information Bull. MR 106, Information Canada (Ottawa)

Buck, W. Keith, and J.F. Henderson, 1962 The role of mineral resources, *in* V.W. Bladen (ed.), *Canadian Population and Northern Colonization*: 109–17

Canada, Department of Energy, Mines and Resources, Geological Survey of Canada, 1970 *Geology and Economic Minerals of Canada*, 5th ed. (Information Canada, Ottawa)

Canada, Department of Energy, Mines and Resources, Mineral Resources Branch *Mineral Yearbook* (Information Canada, Ottawa)

Canada, Department of Finance, 1968 *Public Accounts of Canada* (Ottawa)

Canada, Department of Indian Affairs and Northern Development, Oil and Gas Section, 1968, 1969, 1970 *Oil and Gas North of 60* (Information Canada, Ottawa)

Canada, Department of Indian Affairs and Northern Development, Advisory

Committee on Northern Development, 1970 *Government Activities in the North. 1969 Report and 1970 Plans* (Ottawa): 332 (Egalement en français)

Canada, Department of Indian Affairs and Northern Development, 1970 *Prospectus: North of 60°* (Ottawa)

Canada, Department of National Revenue, 1971 *Corporation Taxation Statistics* (Ottawa)

Canada Yearbook, 1966 (Queen's Printer, Ottawa)

Carr, D.W. and Associates Ltd., 1968 *The Yukon Economy: Its Potential for Growth and Continuity* (Information Canada, Ottawa)

Census of Canada, 1931, 1941, 1951, 1961, 1966

Chang, K.C., 1962 A typology of settlement and community patterns in some circumpolar societies, *Arctic Anthropology*, 1: 28–41

Chrétien, J., 1969 *Speech by the Honourable Jean Chrétien, P.C., M.P., Minister of Indian Affairs and Northern Development: To the Yellowknife Board of Trade*, Yellowknife, N.W.T., 10 Nov.; *To the Council of the Northwest Territories*, Yellowknife, N.W.T., 10 Nov.; *To the Whitehorse Chamber of Commerce, Whitehorse*, Y.T., 11 Nov.; *Before the Yukon Territorial Council*, Whitehorse, Y.T., 12 Nov.

Claval, P., 1970 L'espace en géographie humaine. *Can. Geogr.* XIV, 2: 110–24

Cohen, Maxwell, 1971 The Arctic and the national interest, *International J.*, 26, 1: 52–81

Collie, R.A., 1969 Arctic pipelines, *in* B.F. Sater (ed.), *Arctic and the Middle North Transportation*, 124–6

Collin, A.E., 1963 Waters of the Canadian Arctic Archipelago. *Proc. Arctic Basin Symp., October 1962* (Washington, D.C.), 128–36

Council of the Northwest Territories, 1971 *Debates. Official Report* (Yellowknife), 44: 826

Cowan, I. McT., 1969 Ecology and northern development. *Arctic*, 22, 1 (Mar.): 3–12

Danielson, E.W., 1971 Hudson Bay ice conditions, *Arctic*. 24, 2: 90–107

Day, J.H., and H.M. Rice, 1964 The characteristics of some permafrost soils in the Mackenzie Valley, N.W.T., *Arctic*. XVII, 4: 222–36

Douglas, R.J.W. (ed.), 1970 Geology and economic minerals of Canada, *Geol. Surv. Can. Econ. Geol. Rept.*, 1: 838

Dunbar, M.J., 1966 The sea waters surrounding the Quebec–Labrador peninsula, *Cahiers de géographie de Québec*, 12: 13–35

Dunbar, M., and K.R. Greenaway, 1956 *Arctic Canada from the Air* (Queen's Printer, Ottawa)

Fleming, H.A., 1957 *Canada's Arctic Outlet* (U. Calif. Press, Berkeley)

Gajda, R., 1960 The Canadian ecumene inhabited and uninhabited areas. *Geogr. Bull.*, 15: 5–18

Hall, W.S., 1969 Northern river navigation, as experienced on the Mackenzie watershed of Canada, *in* B.F. Sater (ed.) *Arctic and Middle North Transportation*, 118–21.

Hamelin, L.-E., 1966 Typologie de l'écoumene canadien, *Mémoires de la ciété Royale du Canada*, 4, IV, 1: 41–54. En anglais R.M. Irving (ed.), 1968 *Readings in Canadian Geography* (Toronto), 20–30

— 1968 Un indice circumpolaire, *Annales de Géographie*, 422: 414–30 (voir aussi *North* (Ottawa, 1964), 11, 4: 16–19

— 1969 *Le Canada* (Presses Univ. de France), 304 (édition anglaise en préparation)

— 1970 Un système zonal de primes pour les travailleurs du nord – I, *Cahiers de géographie*, 33: 309–28

Hamelin, L.-E., and F.A. Cook, 1967 *Le périglaciaire par l'image* (Québec)

Hare, F.K., 1959 A photo-reconnaissance survey of Labrador–Ungava, *Geog. Br. Memoir*, 6: 64

— 1964 A policy for geographical research in Canada. *Can. Geogr.*, VIII, 3: 113–16

Hawthorn, H.B. (ed.), 1966, 1967 *A Survey of the Contemporary Indians of Canada: Economic, Political, Educational Needs and Policies Indian Affairs Branch* (Queen's Printer, Ottawa) vol. 1, Oct. 1966; vol. 2, Oct. 1967

Hustich, I., 1968 Finland: a developed and an underdeveloped country, *Acta Geographica*, 20: 155–74

Innis, H.A., and A.R.M. Lower, 1936 *Settlement and the Forest and Mining Frontiers* (Toronto)

Jenness, Diamond, 1955 *Indians of Canada*, 3rd ed. (Queen's Printer, Ottawa)

Judd, D., 1969 Canada's northern policy: retrospect and prospect, *Polar Record*, 14, 92: 593–602

Kierans, Hon. Eric, 1971 Speech on mineral industry taxation in *Debates, House of Commons*, 9 Sept. 1971: 7672–6

Lloyd T., 1959 The geographer as citizen. *Can. Geogr.*, 13: 1–13

— 1970 Canada's Arctic in the age of ecology, *Foreign Affairs*, 48, 4 (July): 721–40.

Lotz, J., 1970 *Northern Realities* (Toronto)

Love, H.W. (ed.), 1966 *The Middle North Symposium* (Montreal)

Mackay, J.R., 1963 The Mackenzie Delta area, N.W.T., *Geogr. Br. Memoir*, 8: 802

— 1971 The origin of massive icy beds in permafrost, western arctic coast, Canada, *Can. J. Earth Sci.*, 8, 4: 397–422

Main, J.R.K., 1961 Transportation as a factor in northern development, *in Background Papers*, Resources for Tomorrow Conference, VI (Queen's Printer), 579–96

Mid-Canada Development Foundation, 1971 *Mid-Canada Report/Rapport sur le Canada-médian* (Toronto)

Mills, W.D., 1971 Government policies regarding economic development in Northern Canada, *The Musk-Ox*, 9: 9–11

Mooney, James, 1928 The aboriginal population of American north of Mexico, *Smithsonian Miscellaneous Collections*, 80, 7

Morton, W.L., 1970   The "North" in Canadian historiography, *Trans. Roy. Soc. Can.* IV, VIII: 31–40

Nicholson, N., 1954   The boundaries of Canada, its provinces and territories, *Geog. Br. Memoir*, no. 2 (Canada Dept. Mines and Technical Surveys, Ottawa)

Northern Science Research Group, *Reports.* Canada, Ministère des Affaires indiennes et du Nord canadien, Ottawa (nombreuses publications depuis 1953)

Ontario Department of Treasury and Economics, Regional Development Branch, 1969   *Northeastern Ontario Regional Development Program, A Progress Report* (Toronto)

— 1969   *Northwestern Ontario Regional Development Program, A Progress Report* (Toronto)

Orvig, S. (ed.), 1970   *Climates of the Polar Regions* (Elsevier, Amsterdam)

Phillips, R.A.J., 1967   *Canada's North.* Macmillan, Toronto

Porsild, A.E., 1957   Illustrated flora of the Canadian Arctic Archipelago, *Nat. Mus. Can. Bull.* 146: 209

Prat, H., 1971   *L'espace multidimensionnel* (Montréal)

Province of Alberta, 1967   *Submission by the Government of Alberta Concerning the Report of the Royal Commission on Taxation* (Queen's Printer, Edmonton)

Québec. 1971   *Rapport de la Commission d'étude sur l'intégrité du Territoire du Québec*, 4, 1: 432 (Rapport H. Dorion)

Rea, K.J., 1968   *The Political Economy of the Canadian North* (Toronto)

Reinelt, E.R. (ed.), 1971   *Proceedings of the Peace-Athabasca Delta Symposium* (Edmonton)

Robins, J.M., 1969   Heavy airfreighting in the Arctic, *in* B.F. Sater (ed.) *Arctic and Middle North Transportation*, 152–8

Robinson, J.L., 1969   *Resources of the Canadian Shield* (Toronto)

Rohmer, R., 1970   *The Green North* (Toronto)

— 1970   Remarks at the opening banquet, in *Essays on Mid Canada*, (Toronto), 101–10

Rousseau, J. (2e. ed.), 1967   *Apercu biogéographique des régions nordiques du Québec* (Québec)

Roy, C., 1971   La chasse des mammifères marins chez les Ivujivimmiut, *Cahiers de Géographie de Québec*, no. 36, 1971 (sous presse)

Royal Society of Canada, 1970   *The Tundra Environment*, 4, VIII, III: 335–412

Santos, M., 1971   *Le métier de géographe en pays sous développé* (Paris)

Sater, J. (ed.), 1969   *The Arctic Basin*, Arctic Institute of North America (Washington)

Sater, B.F. (ed.), 1969   *Arctic and Middle North Transportation*, Arctic Institute of North America (Washington)

Siemens, L.B., 1970   Interdisciplinary research on resource frontier communities, *Aspects of Interdisciplinary Research in Resource Frontier Com-*

munities (Center for Settlement Studies, The University of Manitoba, Winnipeg) 1–34. (Many of the publications of the Center focus upon northern Canadian communities.)

Smith, G.W., 1963   *Territorial Sovereignty in the Canadian North: A Historical Outline to the Problems*, N.C.R.C. 63–7 (Canada, Department of Northern Affairs and Natural Resources, Ottawa)

Statistics Canada, *General Review of the Mineral Industries* (Information Canada, Ottawa, yearly)

Steinmann, A.-P., 1970   Comment peut-on être Esquimau en 1970? *Forces* (Hydro-Quebec), 10: 13–26

Stone, K.H., 1954   Human geographic research in the North American northern lands, *Arctic*, 7, 3, 4: 209–23

Travacon Research Ltd., 1968   *Yukon Transportation Study* (A report prepared for the Department of Indian Affairs and Northern Development, Canada [Ottawa])

Trewartha, G.T., A.H., Robinson, and E.H. Hammond, 1967   *Elements of Geography*, 5th ed. (Toronto)

Underhill, F.H. (ed.), 1959   *The Canadian Northwest: Its Potentialities* (Toronto)

Urquhart, M.C., and K.A.H. Buckley (eds.), 1965   *Historical Statistics of Canada* (Cambridge, England)

Warkentin, J. (ed.), 1967   *Canada* (Methuen Publications); see W.C. Wonders, The Subarctic and forest frontier: 473–507; B. Bird, The Arctic: 508–28 and T. Lloyd, Trends: 583–91

Warnock Hersey International Ltd., 1970   *Arctic Transportation Study* (A report prepared for the Department of Indian Affairs and Northern Development [Ottawa])

Weick, E.R. and C. Merrill, 1969   A look at the future. *North*, XVL, 3 (May-June): 67–77

Whebbel, C.F.J., 1970   Models of political territory. *Proc. Assoc. Am. Geographers*, 2: 152–6

Wonders, W.C., 1960   Postwar settlement trends in the Mackenzie Valley area, *Geografiska Annaler*, XLII, 4: 333–8

— 1962   Our northward course. *Can. Geogr.*, VI, 3–4: 96–105

— 1962   Roads and winter roads in the Mackenzie Valley area. *Occas. Papers*, n. 3, B.C. Div. Can. Assoc. Geographers (Vancouver), 1–19

— 1970   The Canadian Northwest: some geographical perspectives. *Can. Geogr.*, LXXX, 5 (May): 146–65

— 1970   Community and regional development in the North. *Arctic*, 23, 4 (Dec.): 281–4

— (ed. & intro.), 1971   *Canada's Changing North* (Toronto)

Yates, A.B., 1970   Housing programmes for Eskimos in northern Canada, *Polar Record*, 15, 94: 45–50

Zazlow, M., 1971   *The Opening of the Canadian North, 1870–1914* (Toronto)